KENNEDY

REG GADNEY

Holt, Rinehart and Winston
New York

To Margaret Matheson

Copyright © 1983 by Reg Gadney

This book is based on the television film *Kennedy*,
produced by Central Independent Television plc.

Published in the United States by Holt, Rinehart and
Winston, 383 Madison Avenue, New York, New York 10017.

Published simultaneously in Canada by Holt, Rinehart
and Winston of Canada, Limited.

Library of Congress Cataloging in Publication Data.
Gadney, Reg, 1941-
  Kennedy.

  Includes Index.
  1. Kennedy, John F. (John Fitzgerald), 1917-1963.
2. United States – Politics and government – 1961-1963.
3. Presidents – United States – Biography. I. Title.
E842.G23 1983   973.922'092'4 [B]   83-10802

ISBN: 0-03-06 9406-X

First American Edition

This book was designed and produced by
The Rainbird Publishing Group
40 Park Street
London W1Y 4DE

Designer: Martin Bristow
Picture researchers: Tomás Graves and Frances Rowsell
Indexer: P. D. Clark

Printed in Great Britain
10 9 8 7 6 5 4 3 2 1

Contents

Illustration Acknowledgments

The Publishers would like to thank the following for permission to reproduce photographs:

MONOCHROME
Black Star, 104-5 (photo Bob Fitch); 42, 108, 109, 110, 111 (photos Charles Moore).
Camera Press, 20 (photo F. Bachrach); 27 (photo Tom Blau); 116 *right* (photo Edward Clark); 24 (photo Robin Douglas-Home); 11 (photo Robert Jackson/*Dallas Times Herald*); 16 *right*, 158-9 *above*. ©Henri Dauman 1963, 18-9.
John Hillelson Agency, 60, 82, 89 *above*, 92, 132 *below left*, 164 *above right* (photos Cornell Capa/Magnum); 21, 48 (photos Dennis Stock/Magnum); 132-3 *above* (photo Paul Schutzer/Magnum Distribution).
The John F. Kennedy Library, Boston, 1, 15 *left*, 131 *right*; 117 *left and right* (photos Robert Knudsen); 124 *left*, 165 *below* (photos Abbie Rowe); 95, 116 *left*, 164 *above left* (photos Cecil Stoughton).
Keystone Press Agency, 33, 72 *right*, 73, 76, 84-5, 128, 133 *right*, 134 *below left*, 148-9, 157.
Life Magazine ©Time Inc., 115 (photo Edward Clark); 120 *below* (photo Lisa Larsen); 120 *above right* (photo Hy Peskin); 138-9 *below*, 165 *above* (photos Art Rickerby); 69, 70-1 (photos Frank Scherschel); 40-1, 45, 52, 53, 85 *right*, 87, 164 *below right* (photos Paul Schutzer); 37 (photo Hank Walker).
Popperfoto, 8, 9, 10 *above, below left and below right*, 12 *left*, 12-3, 14, 15 *right*, 16 *left*, 28, 29, 32, 38, 40 *left*, 43, 44, 54, 56, 57, 77, 80, 86, 88-9 *below*, 97, 100-1, 121 *left and right*, 124 *right*, 130-1 *above*, 134 *above left and above right*, 145, 150-1, 158-9 *below*, 161 *below*, 168-9, 173.
Photri, 64, 137, 140, 141, 146-7, 152-3.
Rex Features, 136 (photo SIPA Press).
Syndication International, 72 *left*, 120 *above left and above center*.
George Tames/*The New York Times*, 99, 164 *below left*.
Topham Picture Library, 96, 106, 107, 112, 113, 126 *left and right*, 160, 161 *above*, 169 *below*, 172.

COLOR
Associated Press, 39.
Black Star, 102 (photo Art Rickerby); 90 (photo Fred Ward).
Camera Press, 55; 118 *left* (photo Karsh of Ottawa).
The John F. Kennedy Library, Boston, 71 *right*, 163; 75, 78, 91, 94, 130-1 *below*, 143, 155 (photos Robert Knudsen); 22 *left*, 22-3, 26 *above and below*, 31, 114 *above and below*, 119, 135, 158 *below left*, 159 *below right*, 162, 166-7 (photos Cecil Stoughton).
Life Magazine, ©Time Inc., 47 (photo Ralph Crane); 34, 46, 50, 51, 63, 74 (photos Paul Schutzer); 67 (photo George Silk); 171 (photo Dr. Abraham Zapruder).
NASA, 122, 123.
Popperfoto, 58.

Foreword

This illustrated biographical essay is a companion volume to the film for television, *Kennedy*, a dramatization of John F. Kennedy's presidential years.

I owe a special debt of gratitude to the staff of the John Fitzgerald Kennedy Library, Columbia Point, Dorchester, Massachusetts, and a similar debt to the staff of the University Library, Cambridge, England, for their help.

A number of associates of the late President Kennedy, as well as some of his critics, have given me patient and generous guidance and advice. I respect their wish for anonymity but nonetheless wish to record my thanks to them here. I also wish to thank Andrew Brown, Jim Goddard and Christopher Brookeman.

Few Presidents have been so well served by their biographers and historians in the United States and elsewhere. This book – offered as a look back, twenty years later, to the presidential years of JFK – may well be supplemented by a reading of the biographies and memoirs. Of these the following paint either a more detailed or more personal portrait of President Kennedy:

ARTHUR SCHLESINGER JR., *A Thousand Days*. Houghton Mifflin Co., Boston, 1964.

THEODORE SORENSEN, *Kennedy*. Harper & Row, Publishers Inc., New York, 1965.

PIERRE SALINGER, *With Kennedy*. Doubleday & Co., New York, 1966.

WILLIAM MANCHESTER, *The Death of a President*. Harper & Row Publishers Inc., New York, 1967.

BENJAMIN C. BRADLEE, *Conversations with Kennedy*. W. W. Norton & Co., Inc., New York, 1975.

ROBERT F. KENNEDY, *Thirteen Days*. W. W. Norton & Co., Inc., New York, 1969.

HARRIS WOFFORD, *Of Kennedys and Kings*. Farrar, Straus & Giroux, Inc., New York, 1980.

THEODORE H. WHITE, *The Making of the President 1960*. Atheneum Publishers, New York, 1964.

KENNETH P. O'DONNELL, DAVID F. POWERS with JOE MCCARTHY, *Johnny We Hardly Knew Ye*. Little, Brown & Co., Boston, 1972.

ELIE ABEL, *The Missile Crisis*. J. B. Lippincott Co., Philadelphia, 1966.

Two books which tell the story of these years and cover wider general subjects are William Manchester's *The Glory and the Dream* (Little, Brown & Co., Boston, 1974) and David Halberstam's *The Best and the Brightest* (Random House, Inc., New York, 1972).

R. G. 1983

Prologue

Opposite This photograph of Lee Harvey Oswald, President Kennedy's assassin, was exhibit 134 in the Warren Commission's investigation into the assassination. Oswald holds the same rifle that was found in the Texas School Book Depository on November 22, 1963.
Below November 22, 1963, Love Field, Dallas. Lyndon Baines Johnson is sworn in as the thirty-sixth President of the United States by Judge Sarah Hughes. In another part of the presidential jet, Air Force One, lies the casket containing the dead President which had been lifted aboard a few minutes before. The brief ceremony is being recorded by a secretary's tape recorder.

The news of the assassination of America's thirty-fifth President shocked the world. So extraordinary were those hours when we waited to know if John F. Kennedy was really dead – and when we knew, still could not believe it – that now, perhaps, we recall more about what we were doing on Friday, November 22, 1963, and more about ourselves at the time than about Kennedy himself. Our memory of what actually happened on that terrible day has probably been blurred by the span of two decades. Dallas, the city in which Kennedy was assassinated, has taken a different role in the popular imagination and is now celebrated as the title and locale of the world-famous soap opera. Nevertheless, the name of the man to whom the crime has been attributed, Lee Harvey Oswald, remains as notorious as that of any gunman in history.

Details spring to mind charging the memory of the day with high emotion: the President's widow spattered by her husband's blood, Lyndon Johnson taking the presidential oath in the presidential jet

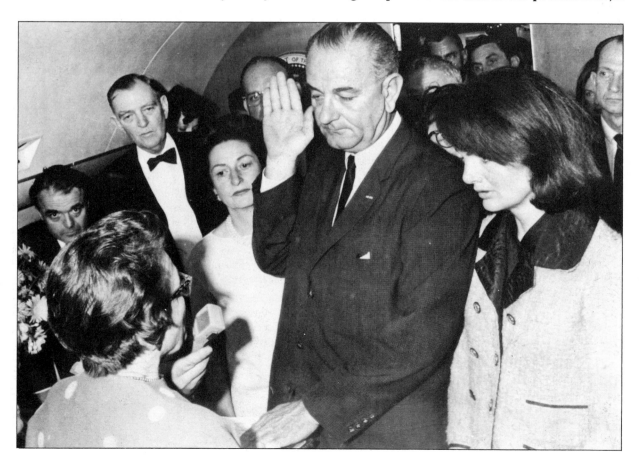

on the runway of Love Field – a fragile moment in history recorded only in photographs and in sound by a secretary's dictating machine. Farther down the plane lay the body of the dead President. Then, two days later, a Dallas night club owner, one Jack Ruby, shot Oswald. The gunman was being transferred to a different jail and was surrounded by seventy police officers in uniform as well as television news cameras when Ruby elbowed his way through the crowd and shot Oswald in the liver with a .38 revolver shouting "You killed the President, you rat!" Oswald died after forty-eight hours in the Parkland Memorial Hospital, tended by doctors among whom were three who had fought to save the life of the President in the same hospital such a short time before. The events of that week in November 1963 seem possessed of a sickly and horrible appropriateness. They contrived during the succeeding years to draw more attention to the nature and circumstances of Kennedy's death than to the spirit of his life. Indeed, they were then compounded by the stories of conspiracy that the ten and a half million words of the Warren Report, the official document of the investigation of Kennedy's assassination, merely seemed to excite still further. *Did Oswald shoot Kennedy? Was there a second gunman? Were two, or three rounds fired, or four? Who might have been behind it all: the CIA, the Soviets, Cuba, the FBI, the Mafia?* The

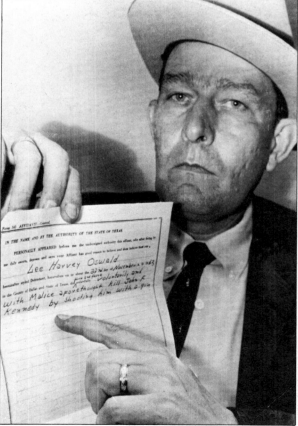

Warren Commission declared that Oswald was the lone gunman. But it offered no clue as to whether or not he was mad, and could suggest no motive. It took persistent speculation about the Kennedy assassination and the further assassinations of Dr. Martin Luther King, Jr., and Robert Kennedy to promote the decision of Congress to establish the ill-titled House Assassinations Committee which announced in 1979 that the President was "probably assassinated as the result of a conspiracy." It held that Oswald was one of the gunmen and went further to suggest that the Mafia and, possibly, anti-Castro gunmen were involved either together or separately. In 1978, an expert in acoustics proposed that four shots had been fired, one of which had come from an angle face-on to the President. This evidence led to the belief that two different gunmen were involved. If this is true, the identity of the other gunman remains unknown.

The committee absolved the FBI and CIA of responsibility but not entirely from blame. The FBI had destroyed documents that had been in Oswald's possession. The CIA had withheld material relating to contact made with Oswald in Moscow by one of its agents. And in a tone of tired regret, the Committee admitted: "The question of Oswald's possible affiliation with military intelligence could not be resolved." There, awkwardly and

Opposite, left A policeman carries a rifle found on the fifth floor staircase of the Texas School Book Depository on November 22, 1963. Nearby were found three empty cartridge cases and the remains of some fried chicken.

Opposite, below Bill Alexander, Dallas County's assistant district attorney, showing the affidavit charging Lee Harvey Oswald with the murder of President Kennedy.

Below Jack Ruby shoots Lee Harvey Oswald dead as Oswald is being transferred from the city prison to the county jail. Subsequently, Ruby declared that he shot Oswald to avenge Jacqueline Kennedy.

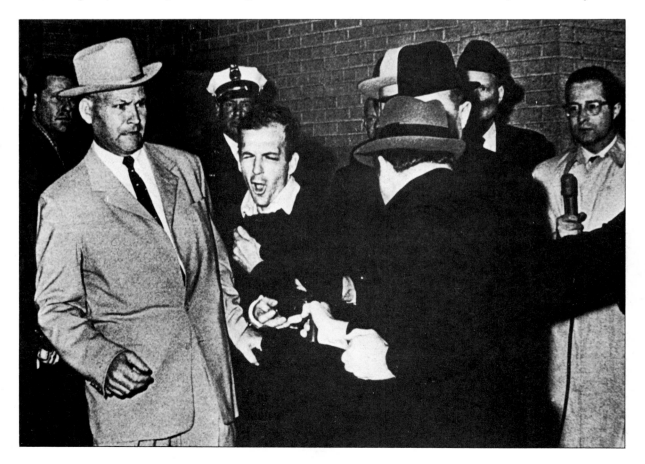

The new President of the United States with Jacqueline Kennedy. Despite the uneasy relationship that existed between the Johnsons and the Kennedys, Lyndon B. Johnson was able to comfort Jacqueline Kennedy.

unsatisfactorily, the case of Lee Harvey Oswald was laid officially to rest. Of those left alive only one man, involuntarily, derived much benefit from the assassination and he was the Vice-President, Lyndon Johnson, who had now become President.

In the intervening years JFK has been mythologized by some. "He was," wrote Theodore White two years after JFK's death, "responsible for much of the myth himself, and his particular style was such as to captivate myth-makers, the men of words and phrases." Kennedy was, of course, a great orator and repeatedly spoke of his generation, a "new" generation, with a persuasive elegance that made people believe he had a sense of vision even if his rhetoric was not always sharply focused. For example, in his State of the Union Message in 1962 he said:

. . . it is the fate of this generation – of you in the Congress and of me as President – to live with a struggle we did not start, in a world we did not make. But the pressures of life are not always distributed by choice. And while no nation has ever faced such a challenge, no nation has ever been so ready to seize the burden and the glory of freedom.

When he was thwarted, most especially in his attempts to remove

The casket containing the body of the dead President is carried into an ambulance at Andrews Air Force Base. Robert Kennedy stands at the back of the truck holding Mrs. Kennedy's hand. Robert and Jacqueline Kennedy accompanied the casket to Bethesda Naval Hospital and then to the White House; Mrs. Kennedy is still in her blood-spattered clothes.

the injustices of exclusion and demonstrable cruelty against American blacks, he could make something elegant and witty out of his frustration.

The United States Government is sitting down at Geneva with the Soviet Union. I can't understand why the city council of Albany, Georgia, cannot do the same for American citizens.

Few Presidents generated such extreme loyalty, such extreme enmity. Sometimes the two extremes themselves became confused:

Two months ago today he died – and a part of America died with him. He was so loving and so beloved, so wise and so courageous, so good and great a man, that we who must carry on his mission shall forever miss him more than we even know.

This was President Johnson's view expressed in spite of the fact that, as Gore Vidal said: "The Kennedys have always been particularly cruel about Johnson, and their personal disdain is reflected and magnified by those around them . . ."

Even so, Jacqueline Kennedy wrote in her own hand to Johnson a letter delivered by hand:

Sunday, November 24, 1963. Jacqueline Kennedy, accompanied by her daughter Caroline, stands by the flag-draped casket, which stands outside the White House.

Dear Mr. President,

Thank you for walking yesterday – behind Jack. You did not have to do that – I am sure many people forbid you to take such a risk – but you did it anyway.

Thank you for your letters to my children. What those letters will mean to them later – you can imagine. The touching thing is, they have always loved you so much, they were most moved to have a letter from you now.

And most of all, Mr. President, thank you for the way you have always treated me – the way you and Lady Bird have always been to me – before, when Jack was alive, and now as President.

. . . we were friends, all four of us. I always thought way before the nomination that Lady Bird should be First Lady – but I don't need to tell you here what I think of her qualities – her extraordinary grace of character – her willingness to assume every burden – She assumed so many for me I love her very much . . . and I love your two daughters . . .

It mustn't be very much help to you your first day in office – to hear children on the lawn at recess. It is just one more example of your kindness that you let them stay – I promise they will soon be gone.

Thank you, Mr. President
Respectfully,
Jackie

JFK's "original contribution to the politics of his time," what Theodore White considered, "the central quality to which we must return," was JFK's "faith in reason . . . Normally, reason is an unattractive quality – it is a dull, gray gnawing at the conscience, or a cold denial of what warm indulgence and craven instinct invite. Kennedy, however, made the quality dance . . ." Vidal was, naturally, more skeptical:

Left Jacqueline Kennedy, with her two children, leaves the Capitol, where the body of President Kennedy lay in state.
Right From the top of Arlington National Cemetery Hill, President Kennedy's funeral procession can be seen heading toward the cemetery over the Memorial Bridge that straddles the Potomac. "He belongs to the country," Jacqueline Kennedy had said expressing her wish for the President to be buried in the National Cemetery at Arlington rather than in the family plot in Massachusetts. Monday, November 25, 1963.

The Kennedys . . . create illusions and call them facts, and between what they are said to be and what they are falls the shadow of all the useful words not spoken, of all the actual deeds not done. But if it is true that in a rough way nations deserve the leadership they get, then a frivolous and apathetic electorate combined with a vain and greedy intellectual establishment will most certainly restore to power the illusion-making Kennedys. Holy family and bedazzled nation, in their faults at least, are well matched.

President Kennedy's Catholicism was an issue in his campaign but it did not diminish his authority as President. He embarked on the Bay of Pigs fiasco. He held firm during the Cuban Missile Crisis. In retrospect, his pursuit of civil rights legislation could have been more committed and so too could his opposition to the growing conflict in Southeast Asia. His Administration did achieve the Nuclear Test Ban Treaty; it did pursue space research – but at enormous financial cost. And, for better or worse, he brought the style of a new generation to the White House. No other political family in this century has excited so much interest.

JFK was not America's youngest President – Theodore Roosevelt was a year younger when he succeeded McKinley in 1901 – but he was the youngest *elected* President and when he died he seemed by very far the youngest of the world's leaders. Indeed, twenty years after his death, he still seems fixed in the mind as a young man and it is strange to think that, had he lived, he would today be sixty-six years old. Had he been reelected in 1964 he would, at the expiration of his second term of office in 1968, have been fifty-one. The temptation to speculate on what would have happened had he not gone to Texas is great. But he went.

Chapter 1

Dallas: November 22, 1963

. . . the guerillas, saboteurs, insurgents and assassins who threaten freedom in a less direct but equally dangerous manner . . .

We in this country, in this generation, are, by destiny rather than choice, the watchmen on the walls of world freedom. We ask, therefore, that we may be worthy of our power and responsibility, that we may exercise our strength with wisdom and restraint, and that we may achieve in our time and for all time the ancient vision of "peace on earth, good will toward men." That must always be our goal – and the righteousness of our cause must always underlie our strength. For as was written long ago: "Except the Lord keep the city, the watchman waketh but in vain." (from John F. Kennedy's undelivered speech for the Dallas Citizens Council released to the press November 22, 1963)

On the morning of Friday, November 22, 1963, six members of Kennedy's Cabinet were bound for Tokyo in a presidential jet, Aircraft 86972. Dean Rusk, Secretary of State; Orville Freeman, Secretary of Agriculture; Luther Hodges, Secretary of Commerce; Douglas Dillon, Secretary of the Treasury; Willard Wirtz, Secretary of Labor; and Stewart Udall, Secretary of the Interior were accompanied by their wives and staff. The President's Press Secretary, Pierre Salinger, and his wife, Nancy, were also with them. The previous evening they had said farewell to Robert McNamara, Secretary of Defense, and McGeorge Bundy, Special Assistant to the President for National Security Affairs. McNamara

Left Among President Kennedy's advisors, Dean Rusk usually proved less decisive than Robert McNamara whose previous job had been chief executive of the Ford Motor Company. This photograph shows *(left to right)* Secretary of State Rusk, JFK, and Secretary of Defense McNamara, January 23, 1961.
Right JFK with McGeorge Bundy, Special Assistant for National Security Affairs. Bundy had previously been dean of the Faculty of Arts and Sciences at Harvard.

and Bundy returned to Washington after depressing talks in Hawaii with the U.S. Ambassador to Saigon, Henry Cabot Lodge, and General Paul D. Harkins. The situation in Vietnam was worsening. Only two weeks before, President Ngo Dinh Diem had been thrown out of office by a military coup and, along with his brother, had been assassinated. The trust between Kennedy and Diem had already been fractured. Kennedy had become disenchanted with Diem's administration and had decided he was no longer prepared to squander U.S. war supplies on him. Diem preferred to spend time and money warring with the Buddhists rather than with the Vietcong and North Vietnamese. Indeed, there were strong hints that the Kennedy Administration had connived in the coup that precipitated Diem's assassination. In Washington the coup was accepted as more or less unavoidable. The strongest regret at Diem's fate was felt by Lyndon Johnson. Lodge told McNamara and Bundy that the Vietcong were in a much stronger position than had been generally assumed. He was going to go to Washington to warn Kennedy. He now felt that the U.S. Government was supporting a cause well-nigh lost. But when he reached San Francisco he heard what had happened in Dallas. Kennedy never heard the warning.

Salinger, unlike Dean Rusk and the other members of the Cabinet in the presidential jet, was not going to Tokyo for discussions on trade. Salinger's mission was a different one. Kennedy had asked him to sound out the Japanese about a state visit to Japan for February 1964. The last presidential visit, by Eisenhower, had been an embarrassment to both sides, and had led to violent riots. Kennedy intended the 1964 Japanese visit to be part of a tour he would make with his wife, taking in the Philippines, Pakistan, and India as well, and he told Kenneth O'Donnell, Special Assistant to the President for appointments, that he might even bring the tour forward.

The presidential aircraft took off from Honolulu just before breakfast. The passengers settled down for the day-long flight that would be punctuated only by a single stop for refueling at Wake Island. After takeoff, in the clear sky, one observer said that "Oahu looked like a fresh salad in mint aspic." It was, by all accounts, a beautiful day, and everyone was feeling in good spirits. The wives discussed shopping plans for their time in Japan; the husbands and staff began to sift through their papers in preparation for the trade talks. There were complex issues involved and the papers were heavy going.

Shortly after breakfast, Pierre Salinger saw the Assistant Secretary of State, Robert Manning, come down the aisle towards him from the direction of the forward cabin. Manning told Salinger that Dean Rusk would like to see him up front. Salinger followed Manning forward and noticed that the wives of the senior Cabinet members had been moved to a different section of the aircraft. When Salinger reached the forward cabin Rusk said that before beginning what he had to say, he would wait for Walter Heller,

Chairman of the Council for Economic Advisers, and Myer Feldman from the President's Special Counsel Office and an expert on business affairs. Rusk was clearly very agitated but fighting to control himself. Prompted by natural curiosity as to the cause of Rusk's agitation and by his bafflement at being called to such an unexpected meeting, Salinger looked at the teletyped UPI bulletin. He read:

```
UPI A7N DA
        PRECEDE KENNEDY
    DALLAS, NOV. 22  UPI – THREE SHOTS WERE FIRED AT PRESIDENT KENNEDY'S
MOTORCADE TODAY IN DOWNTOWN DALLAS
JT1234PCS..
```

Rusk then read out in his even baritone voice two more bulletins announcing that the President had possibly been seriously wounded, perhaps even fatally, by an assassin's bullet.

Luther Hodges was so shocked he was on the point of collapse but Willard Wirtz tried to reassure himself and his colleagues by pointing out how garbled the bulletins were.

The plane had now been airborne for just over two hours.

For some seconds all of them were silent while the jet swept on above high white cloud banks.

"We have got to turn back," Salinger said, ". . . turn back. Now."

Rusk hesitated, unable to accept the truth of what he had read.

He said: "We ought to have some confirmation." Perhaps it was an exaggeration, even a mistake. After all, it was only a press report.

Salinger went to the two Signal Corps sergeants, Walter Baughman and Darrel Skinner. He told them to put him in immediate contact with the White House Situation Room. In less than a minute Commander Oliver Hallett came up on the air. Salinger found that he was unable to remember the secret communications code. He could only remember his own U.S. Secret Service White House Communications Agency Code: Wayside.

"Wayside . . . Situation. What is the information on the President?"

From Washington, Hallett told Salinger that he too was seeking confirmation of the reports from Dallas. As far as he knew the President had been shot.

"Where?"

"In the head."

"And, is he –?"

"At this moment, yes, we believe he is alive."

"Okay."

Salinger had been repeating what Hallett was saying word for word so that the others could follow the conversation.

Rusk looked at his colleagues inquiringly.

"We have to turn round," Douglas Dillon said. The issue of whether to go on or turn back was debated for some thirty seconds.

Then Rusk decided. They would go back immediately. Rusk gave the order to return.

Word was sent to Admiral Harry D. Felt to have a Boeing 707 ready for take-off at Honolulu to carry Rusk, Manning and Salinger direct to Dallas. Everyone else would go back to Washington on the presidential jet after refueling. As yet, no one in the plane knew whether the President was alive or dead. Thirty-five thousand feet above the Pacific the jet turned around.

Salinger stayed in the communications cabin with the line open to the White House. Every half minute he asked for more information, his large sensitive face turned towards the window.

(Left to right) Pierre Salinger, White House Press Secretary; Orville L. Freeman, Secretary of Agriculture; C. Douglas Dillon, Secretary of Treasury; Dean Rusk, Secretary of State; Stewart L. Udall, Secretary of the Interior; Luther H. Hodges, Secretary of Commerce, on their arrival back in the United States after their aborted trip to Tokyo, November 22, 1963.

Friday, November 22 was a magnificent fall day on the East Coast of America. On Cape Cod the light was golden, the sea still and luminous. In the gardens of the Kennedy family houses at Hyannis Port remnants of fall flowers were still in bloom around the well-tended lawns: asters, chrysanthemums, marigolds, calendulas, black-eyed susans and roses. Hyannis Port is no more than a scramble of seaside houses and cottages used mainly in the summer. Hyannis, a village east of Hyannis Port, is nearby and one of the most fashionable of vacation retreats in Barnstable County. The houses at Hyannis Port are by no means the grandest of America's summer homes, but for many years they have been used by the wealthy families of Massachusetts, especially the rich Boston-Irish. The Kennedys had first come here in 1928, to the houses at the bottom of Scudder Avenue on the water's edge. Jack Kennedy bought one next door and sometime later Bobby Kennedy bought one too. The three houses, all on the same grassy area, are separated by hedges and form what became known as the Kennedy

The family of Joseph and Rose Kennedy at Hyannis Port in the summer of 1934, six years after moving there. *(Left to right, standing)* Joe, Jr., who was killed in World War II; Kathleen or "Kick" who was killed in a plane accident in 1948; JFK *(seated)*; Rosemary; Eunice, later Mrs. Sargent Shriver. *(Left to right, seated)* Patricia, later Mrs. Peter Lawford; Robert; Rose; Joseph with Edward ("Teddy") in his lap; Jean, later Mrs. Stephen Smith.

JFK, Caroline and Jacqueline in the
Kennedy compound, Hyannis Port.

compound. The natives of Hyannis Port and, indeed, of Hyannis
itself considered the Kennedys to be outsiders and, after 1960,
received the world's reporters and cameramen, Secret Service
people, staff, and sightseers with no particular pleasure. Indeed,
the Civic Committee had made strong protests. Shortly after her
husband's nomination, Jacqueline Kennedy ordered a bare wooden
fence to be constructed to make sightseeing rather more difficult. It
did not deter the crowds who came to gawk, and JFK thought the
fence ought not to be extended all around the compound. So, once
his own house, which is only four yards from the road, had been
surrounded, he called a halt to its construction.

Joseph P. Kennedy, the family patriarch, had been anxious
about the weather during the morning, for his niece, Ann Gargan,
was flying to see relatives in Detroit that afternoon. Earlier in the
morning the thick autumn mist across Nantucket Sound held fast.
Before noon it lifted, so flights were not delayed after all. Ann
would be able to spend Thanksgiving at her sister's house, and then
travel down to Palm Beach to spend Christmas with the Kennedys
there. The rest of the Kennedys would be here at Hyannis Port for
Thanksgiving. There were to be birthday celebrations for John, the
President's son who would be three on November 25. On
November 27, Caroline would be six and they were also going to
celebrate the anniversary of JFK's victory in the 1960 election.
Joseph yearned for his son to come to Hyannis Port. Then he could
gaze out from his rooms on the second floor at the presidential
trailer from the White House which would be lined up next to
JFK's house. Two weeks had passed since he had last seen his son.
It had been a memorable farewell. On that Sunday evening, the
President's helicopter had set down on the lawn in the compound.
JFK had kissed his father good-bye, touched the old man's
half-paralyzed face, and said he looked forward to seeing him for
Thanksgiving, after the Texas trip.

Left John Kennedy, Jr. with his father aboard a helicopter between Hyannis Port and Otis Air Force Base, Massachusetts. **Below** JFK bids his father farewell in his customary manner. On the left is Ann Gargan, a cousin of JFK's, who cared devotedly for Joseph Kennedy after his stroke.

When his son had left the room, the old man, unable to speak anymore as a result of a stroke, signaled to his nurse to have him carried to the window so he could watch the departure of his son's helicopter. He was lifted from his bed and wheeled to the balcony that faced the lawn. He stared at the helicopter, its blades whirring, the air currents beating down the flowers around the lawns. Then, without warning, the President reappeared, crouched down, and kissed his father on the forehead. It was the last time they saw each other.

On the morning of November 22, Joseph Kennedy read *The New York Times* while his wife, Rose, went to Mass. Earlier he had undergone physiotherapy in his indoor swimming pool. At lunch

there were just Ann Gargan and Rose to keep him company. After lunch he was taken back to his bed and fell asleep. Rose Kennedy also took a nap, the curtains shut to keep out the bright sun. Outside the house, Ann Gargan stood with Joseph Kennedy's nurse, Rita Dallas, watching her suitcases being placed in the car that would take her to the airport for the Detroit plane.

It was then that the routine at the Hyannis Port compound was dramatically broken. One of the maids yelled out to the two women standing by the car that the President had been shot.

It was also a warm day at Hickory Hill, Robert Kennedy's house at McLean, Virginia. RFK and his wife, Ethel, Robert Morgenthau, U.S. Attorney for New York's Southern District, and Silvio Mollo, Morgenthau's deputy, were at lunch beside the Hickory Hill swimming pool. Here too the sky was clear and the atmosphere autumnal. The beech and maple trees were almost bare, and there was a gentle haze across the hills. The lunch was a Kennedy Friday lunch: clam chowder, tunafish sandwiches, and coffee. The conversation was mainly about the meeting the three men had just come from, a discussion about the Attorney General's continuing war against organized crime.

Ethel and Robert Kennedy at Hickory Hill, their home in McLean, Virginia.

The alfresco lunch was almost over and the Attorney General looked at his watch and suggested that he and his two colleagues go back to work. It was at this moment, at about 1:45 P.M., that some men, painting an extension to the house, began to shout that the President had been shot. Simultaneously, the telephone by the pool rang. Ethel Kennedy took it and found herself talking to the Director of the Federal Bureau of Investigation, J. Edgar Hoover. He wanted to speak to the Attorney General. It was only in emergencies that Hoover called Robert Kennedy at home.

Arthur Schlesinger later recorded Bobby Kennedy's own version of what Hoover said:

"I have news for you. The President's been shot"; or "I have news for you" and I might have said, "What?" and he said "The President's been shot." And – well, I don't know what I said – probably "Oh" or something – and I don't know whether he then – I asked him or got into whether it was serious, and I think he said, "I think it's serious". . . He said, "I'll call you back. . . when I find out more." I don't remember anything more of that conversation.

Robert replaced the white telephone receiver and walked back to Ethel and the two guests with his hand across his mouth and in a state of great distress.

Ethel Kennedy held him in her arms and comforted him. He was in no doubt about what to do next. He had to leave at once for his brother's side. He went back to the house and sent out instructions to Robert McNamara to make a plane available to fly to Dallas.

Edward Kennedy, the thirty-one-year-old Senator from Massachusetts and the youngest of the Kennedy brothers, was presiding over a debate in the Senate. The chamber was half full and not a great deal of attention was being paid to the speech of the Republican Senator from Vermont, Winston Prouty. His subject that early afternoon was federal library services and Edward Kennedy was half listening to Prouty while signing letters. In the press gallery, a press liaison officer, Richard Riedel, read the Associated Press teletypes:

> BULLETIN
> DALLAS, NOV.22(AP) -- PRESIDENT KENNEDY WAS
> SHOT TODAY JUST AS HIS MOTORCADE LEFT DOWN-
> TOWN DALLAS. MRS. KENNEDY JUMPED UP AND
> GRABBED MR. KENNEDY. SHE CRIED, "OH, NO!"
> THE MOTORCADE SPED ON.

Riedel, who had worked at the Senate for fifty years, ran on to the floor of the Senate. "The President . . . !" he whispered to Senator Spessard Holland from Florida. "He's been shot." And he repeated the news to Senator Wayne Morse from Oregon who was supervising the passage of the bill Prouty was still speaking about. Then Riedel saw Teddy Kennedy and went to the rostrum. No one had intervened in a debate in this manner before.

Left JFK, John, Jr., Jacqueline, and
Caroline at Hyannis Port, August 14, 1963.
Below Few Presidents showed their love for
their children so publicly.

Senator Kennedy looked down at Riedel.

Riedel said, "Your brother . . ."

"Yes?"

"The President. Your brother . . . he's been shot . . ."

Senator Holland was by now crossing the floor to the rostrum. Teddy Kennedy asked Riedel if he was sure of what he was saying. By now the noise in the Senate was rising and Prouty stopped talking. Edward Kennedy collected the signed and unsigned letters together and made for the press gallery and the teletype machines. When he got there the crowd of journalists and Senate workers prevented him from getting near the bulletins. He made his way alone to the Vice-President's office and sat down at Johnson's desk to start telephoning. He could not get through to Robert, the lines were either busy or dead.

He left Johnson's office at a run and outside the building he got a lift to the old Senate Office Building where he had his office. Here, by chance, he met up with an old Harvard friend, Claude Hooten, who had come to Washington from Houston because that night Edward and Joan Kennedy were holding a dinner to celebrate their fifth wedding anniversary.

Everyone seemed to be straining to make sense of the cacophony of news coming from portable radios. In his office Edward once again tried to get through to the Attorney General's office at the

Robert Kennedy as Attorney General, in his office at the Department of Justice in Washington.

Department of Justice but the lines had gone dead. Eventually a White House telephone operator told him that his brother, the Attorney General, was in the middle of a long call to Dallas. Edward now sought out another Harvard friend, speech-writer Milton Gwirtzman. Together with Hooten and Gwirtzman, Teddy Kennedy drove in Gwirtzman's Mercedes to Georgetown to find Joan Kennedy, who was having her hair done for the anniversary dinner and had not heard the news.

Caroline and John Kennedy, two of the most famous children in the world, were self-possessed and lively. Caroline's devotion was to her parents and her pets; John's was to his parents and the presidential helicopters. Tonight, Caroline was going to spend her first night away from home with the family of her friend, Agatha Pozen. Agatha's mother, Liz, was at the White House to collect Caroline and take her to their home on Raymond Street. The car would be followed discreetly by a Secret Service agent. The two cars pulled away. The girls with Liz Pozen were so excited she thought she would turn on the radio to calm them down. When she switched it on she found that the usual program had been interrupted with news flashes from Dallas. The Secret Service driver tailing her had also heard the news on the radio and drew up

Below JFK is greeted by John and Caroline at Otis Air Force Base, August 23, 1963. **Opposite** A week before his father's assassination John Kennedy, Jr., marches into the presidential limousine. The President has just placed a wreath on the graves of the Unknown Soldiers in a Veterans Day ceremony, November 13, 1963.

level with Liz Pozen's car. Out of the children's hearing, they discussed what to do. It was obvious that something terrible had happened but it was still not certain what it was. The Secret Service man radioed the White House and asked for orders and over the radio the news of the shooting was confirmed. In an agony of doubt as to what might be the best thing to do and unable to get a clear picture of what was going on, the Secret Service man told Mrs. Pozen he was taking Caroline back to the White House. He bundled Caroline, with her small suitcase and her teddy bear, into his car and sped back to the White House. Caroline had missed her first night away from a home that very soon would not be home anymore.

It was a dime telephone call from a phone booth in the hall of the Parkland Memorial Hospital in Dallas by the wife of a United Press International employee that sent the teletypes clattering out the message that was to stun the world. It read:

FLASH

PRESIDENT KENNEDY DEAD

JT135PCS

The presidential jet carrying Rusk and the other members of the Cabinet had by now been ordered back to Washington with no stop at Dallas. It was 1:35 P.M. in Dallas, 2:35 P.M. in Washington. Salinger had kept radio communications open. Now the words came. He told Rusk, who spoke over the intercom: "The President is dead. I am saddened to have to tell you this grievous news. We have a new President. May God bless our nation and our new President." Pierre Salinger, weeping unashamedly, found his way back to his wife, Nancy. She stood up and held him in her arms.

Rose Kennedy, at Hyannis Port, sought solace in prayer and solitude. She did not want her husband told. Not yet. He was still asleep in his bedroom. She left the house and walked across the lawns to the sand dunes. A slight wind had risen. The tough dune grass was being blown about in the wind. She stood there alone and gazed out across Nantucket Sound.

Bobby Kennedy was told by Secret Service agent, Clint Hill, in a call from Dallas, that the President was dead. A few moments later, J. Edgar Hoover rang to tell him what he already knew. The calls to Hickory Hill continued. Lyndon Johnson called and asked him, as Attorney General, how he could have himself sworn in as President. Kennedy made a few inquiries, rang back, and told the new President that anybody could do it. A district court judge, maybe.

Caroline and John were at the White House with Nancy Tuckerman, the White House social secretary; Maud Shaw, the children's English nanny; Toni and Ben Bradlee, who was then chief of *Newsweek's* Washington Bureau. Agatha Pozen had been brought back to the White House to keep Caroline company. Neither of the

Caroline and John take afternoon tea on the South Lawn of the White House with their English nurse, Maud Shaw. April 1, 1963.

children had been told their father was dead. Who should tell them? Who among friends and White House staff could bring himself to do it? The adults watched the children playing on the carpet and just before five o'clock, conversation was drowned out by the roar of a helicopter on the South Lawn. John and Caroline ran across the room to look out the windows, crying out in delight: "Mommy! Daddy! Daddy is here! Mommy and Daddy are home!"

Chapter 2

Election: November 8, 1960

History will not judge our endeavors, and a government cannot be selected merely on the basis of color or creed or even party affiliation. Neither will competence and loyalty and stature, while essential to the utmost, suffice in times such as these.

For of those to whom much is given, much is required. And when at some future date the high court of history sits in judgment on each of us, recording whether in our brief span of service we fulfilled our responsibilities to the state, our success or failure, in whatever office we hold, will be measured by the answers to four questions:

First, were we truly men of courage, with the courage to stand up to one's enemies, and the courage to stand up, when necessary, to one's associates, the courage to resist public pressure as well as private greed?

Second, were we truly men of judgment, with perceptive judgment of the future as well as of the past, of our own mistakes as well as the

Opposite John F. Kennedy, then a senator, returns to his office at the Capitol, with Jacqueline, after an operation on his spine. May 1955.

Below JFK is swamped by confetti and paper streamers as his motorcade moves up Broadway in downtown Los Angeles on November 1, 1960. His energetic and highly personal style brought a new intensity to American political campaigning.

JFK at a penthouse hideaway during the 1960 Democratic convention in Los Angeles.

mistakes of others, with enough wisdom to know what we did not know, and enough candor to admit it?

Third, were we truly men of integrity, men who never ran out on either the principles in which we believed or the people who believed in us, men whom neither financial gain nor political ambition could ever divert from the fulfillment of our sacred trust?

Finally, were we truly men of dedication, with an honor mortgaged to no single individual or group and compromised by no private obligation or aim, but devoted solely to serving the public good and the national interest?

Courage, judgment, integrity, dedication – these are the historic qualities of the Bay Colony and the Bay State, the qualities which this State has consistently sent to Beacon Hill here in Boston and to Capitol Hill back in Washington. And these are the qualities which, with God's help, this son of Massachusetts hopes will characterize our government's conduct in the four stormy years that lie ahead. Humbly I ask His help in this undertaking: but aware that on earth His will is worked by men, I ask for your help and your prayers as I embark on this new and solemn journey.

(from John F. Kennedy's address, as President-elect, to the Massachusetts State Legislature, January 9, 1961)

John Fitzgerald Kennedy, known variously to his intimates and others as Jack, Johnny or JFK and to everyone as President Kennedy, spent the election night of November 8, 1960 in the Kennedy compound in Hyannis Port surrounded by his family and aides.

The night before, rounding off his campaign with his supporters in the Boston Garden, he had said:

I thank you for your past support. I ask you to join us tomorrow. And, most of all, I ask you to join us in all the tomorrows yet to come, in building America, moving America, picking this country of ours up and sending it into the sixties.

The next day the largest number of popular votes in any American election were cast: 68,832,818, just over one-tenth more than had been cast four years before when Eisenhower beat Stevenson by a margin of 9,852,238 popular votes and received 86.06 percent of the electoral votes. Four years after in 1960, the margin would look very different.

On the morning of November 8, 1960, together with his wife, JFK voted for himself in Boston. He gave his address as 122 Bowdoin Street, Boston. Afterwards the couple flew from Boston to Hyannis Port and the shelter of the compound. There was touch football with Bobby and Teddy and the Kennedy wives and sisters on the lawn. Jacqueline, thirty-one years old, was expecting a baby in three weeks. She lunched alone with JFK and spent the day resting. JFK relaxed briefly from 3:30 P.M. but grew understandably restless and by 5:00 P.M. he had joined his brothers and his aides to start the long wait for the returns.

The campaign of the previous months had forged its own bitterness and comedy. In August, James Reston reported in *The New York Times:*

WASHINGTON, Aug. 16 – The Democrats are far from happy about the current phase of the campaign.

Their Presidential nominee, Senator John F. Kennedy, has not only fallen behind Vice-President Nixon in the first nationwide poll since the conventions – 44 percent to 50 for Nixon, with 6 percent undecided – but has lost his voice.

Soon after, the gap closed, and during September both candidates stood even in the polls, though those who could not decide had increased to 7 percent. In September Nixon was ahead with 49 percent to Kennedy's 46 percent. After an especially difficult session of Congress for Johnson, which Reston reported on August 16, the poll fluctuated and the margin remained perilously narrow for both candidates. The Republicans continued to harass Kennedy and Johnson in the Senate. Even in August 1960 it looked as though the Democrats had an almost impossible task on their hands, seeking to increase the minimum wage, legislate on housing and introduce federal assistance for education and medical care for the old. Nixon said the campaign would yield an unprecedentedly close result. In that he was right; in virtually everything else he was wrong. Two factors Nixon was aware of: the first was the persuasive power of television – now, more than forty million families in America possessed television sets; second, across America a new wave of increasingly prosperous Americans had moved from inner cities into the suburbs. The latter phenomenon assisted Nixon because, as people owned more and better property and enjoyed a better standard of living, they tended, having more to lose, to become more conservative in their views.

Nixon realized that the proposal that the two presidential candidates should debate on television was not to his advantage.

. . . I knew [he said in his memoirs] that the debates would benefit Kennedy more than me by giving his views national exposure, which he needed more than I did. Further, he would have the tactical advantage of being on the offensive. . . . The question we faced was not whether to debate, but how to arrange the debates so as to give Kennedy the least possible advantage.

Kennedy realized, Theodore Sorensen, wrote later, that his style ". . . was ideally suited to this medium. His unadorned manner of delivery, his lack of gestures and dramatic inflections, his slightly shy but earnest charm, may all have been handicaps on the hustings, but they were exactly right for the living room. He had seen in West Virginia tiny ramshackle shacks with no plumbing, and no newspapers or magazines but with large television aerials." Their inhabitants would hear him; above all, they would see him.

Both men had to grab the advantage of television exposure and make the most of it. Kennedy's strategy — and "strategy" was a

JFK in 1960, campaigning in West Virginia among the miners.

Left The Democratic presidential nominee, with Jacqueline, boards the yacht *Marlin* for a cruise on Nantucket Sound, November 19, 1960.
Opposite JFK at the Democratic convention in Los Angeles in 1960.

favorite Kennedy word — was conceived by a group of his advisors headed by Robert Kennedy. He would build up a broad base and from it snipe elegantly at Nixon.

The Kennedys sought out the younger voters, the factory workers, the liberals. Lyndon Johnson was to secure and build upon the Democratic bases in the southern states. Kennedy needed to win Texas, California, Illinois, and Michigan, as well as the industrial areas of the Northeast whose votes were so vital to his campaign. If he could gain those states he would only need another 32 out of the 269 electoral votes to give him victory. Aided by his academic friends from Harvard and Yale and the energies of his

Left JFK, RFK and Ted in July 1960. JFK's brothers played an active part in the presidential campaign. RFK in particular provided the presidential candidate with invaluable political advice and was his campaign manager.
Below JFK with Richard M. Nixon at the time of the television debates between the two presidential candidates in October, 1960. Kennedy owed a substantial measure of his success in the election to his appearances on television. His image and style proved far more acceptable to viewers than Nixon's.

political campaign experts, especially Kenny O'Donnell and Larry O'Brien, as well as the steely organizational ability of his brother Robert, he set off on a campaign in large part made possible by the wealth of his father. Kennedy's main handicaps were, first, that he appeared far younger than Nixon, even though the actual difference in their ages was only four years, and second, that his father's political reputation was tainted because as American Ambassador in Britain he had advocated appeasement and as a result had fallen out of favor. Third, he was a Roman Catholic.

Nixon's strategy was to campaign in forty-three states, to watch the rise and fall of the polls, and to manipulate the popular vote. He would trade on his experience as Vice-President with the doubtful support of Eisenhower. Ike was asked by a journalist how many major decisions his Vice-President had taken part in during his administration. "If you give me a week," Eisenhower told his amused audience, "I might think of one."

Almost at once things went awry for Nixon. He hurt his knee and had to rest for two weeks. He had only just recovered from this mishap when he caught flu, his temperature rising to 103 degrees. It seemed as though he was now campaigning like a long-distance runner with a limp. And Kennedy's brilliant quips cannot have helped:

In California:

QUESTIONER: Senator, when does the moratorium end on Nixon's hospitalization and your ability to attack him?
JFK: Well, I said I would not mention him unless I could praise him until he got out of the hospital, and I have not mentioned him.

In New York:

JFK: The man in the audience said that I should tell Mr. Nixon that experience is what he will have left after this campaign is over. I don't know why we never think of these things.

Mr. Nixon may be very experienced in kitchen debates, but so are a great many other married men I know.

There are children in Africa named Thomas Jefferson, George Washington and Abraham Lincoln. There are none called Lenin, or Trotsky or Stalin – or Nixon.

Then came the television debates. Seventy million people watched the first one on September 26, 1960. Most of them probably looked and did not listen too hard. They saw Kennedy smiling, serious, hard, charming, cool. They saw Nixon with a shirt too large for him, round-shouldered, glum and his face plastered with make-up

to hide his apparently ill-shaven jowls. He also sweated. His own commentary on his performance is revealing, a blend of truthful observation and self-pity:

It is a devastating commentary on the nature of television as a political medium that what hurt me the most in the first debate was not the substance of the encounter between Kennedy and me, but the disadvantageous contrast in our physical appearances. After the program ended, callers, including my mother, wanted to know if anything was wrong, because I did not look well.

By the last of the four debates, on October 21, twenty million fewer Americans bothered to tune in than the seventy million who had watched on September 26. Nixon described the nonwatchers as "stubborn." Gallup found that 49 percent were now for Kennedy and 46 percent for Nixon. Then came the struggle for the black vote. Nixon's running mate, Henry Cabot Lodge said that it was part of the Republican program to have "a Negro in the Cabinet." Nixon contradicted him. On October 19, Martin Luther King was sentenced to four months hard labor in Atlanta. Nixon was asked if he had a view about it and said that he did not. Kennedy, on the other hand, telephoned Coretta King personally. Robert Kennedy spoke to the judge who had pronounced sentence.

The support offered by JFK and RFK to Martin Luther King, Jr., (shown here with Mrs. King shortly after his arrest in 1960) was a decisive factor in gaining the support of black voters. During Kennedy's presidency, King made himself the spiritual leader of the majority of America's black population.

JFK confers with his campaign manager in Los Angeles, July 10, 1960.

The next day, Martin Luther King walked out of jail on bail. Coretta King told the story to her friends and eventually it became public knowledge – a crucial factor in Kennedy's continuing campaign for black support.

By the night of November 8 it was anyone's guess who would win. The family gathered to await the results. They were all there together: JFK and Jackie, RFK and Ethel, Joe and Rose, Teddy and Joan, Peter and Pat Kennedy Lawford, Sargent and Eunice Kennedy Shriver, Stephen and Jean Kennedy Smith.

RFK had established a communications center in the sun room of his house in the compound. This was where the news would come in. There were thirty telephones, four wire service teletypes, and a bank of televisions. The telephones were manned by some sixteen campaign workers, mostly middle-aged women. Throughout the evening JFK moved between the communications center, his own house where Jackie was resting and his parents' house where he talked with his father and mother.

The first news came from CBS's IBM computer, which forecast shortly after 7:00 P.M. that the odds on a Nixon win were running at a hundred to one. Guesswork was swept away by news of actual results. Kennedy won Connecticut with a 90,000 vote majority, a fine win; but then Connecticut was near to home. Yet, it was a sign of how the northern industrial states would go. Between 8:00 and 9:00 P.M. there were indications from Philadelphia and Chicago that some 75 percent of the vote was going to Kennedy. This was the sort of scoring he needed to resist the pressure of the rural areas that would be Republican. Nixon held fast in the South, making advances in Kentucky and Tennessee. But then he tripped up in North and South Carolina and these were the states that Nixon had aimed to win. Moreover, it seemed that black voters who had been with Eisenhower in 1956 were changing their allegiance and going with Kennedy. The tide for Kennedy continued between nine and ten o'clock. Kennedy might even expect a win by 600,000 votes in Chicago. New York was turning to Kennedy. By 11:00 P.M. the forecast was that Kennedy would win by a popular vote of over a million. It looked as though it was settled when only 21 percent of the national vote had been counted. Then Nixon won in Oklahoma and Virginia, and he won in areas of New Jersey, even in Hudson County, a Catholic stronghold. Kennedy was only slightly ahead in Wisconsin and Michigan. It began to look as though Nixon was coming up fast from behind.

That was the impression given by the Republican National Chairman, Thruston B. Morton, who was quoted as saying:

"It's going to be all right. We've got this thing, and I know we're going to celebrate if we have to carry on here until the dawn kills

JFK and Jacqueline campaigning on Broadway, New York, in October 1960.

In the 1960 campaign, JFK campaigned to the point of exhaustion. His right hand became swollen as a result of shaking the hands of well-wishers.

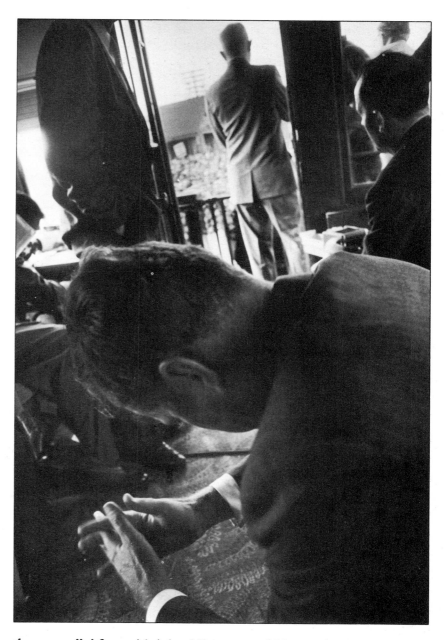

the moon." After midnight, Nixon won Ohio, a win that especially wounded Kennedy, who had campaigned there six times, and where a woman squeezed his hand so hard it actually bled.

Throughout the long night JFK remained anxious and concerned. In the communications center, wins were greeted with boisterous applause, sometimes a whoop. The three brothers were less than jubilant. All was not going according to plan. The win, if and when it came, would be terribly narrow. Upstairs, Lou Harris worked and reworked his slide rule. The narrowness of the margins made certain prediction almost impossible. A few minutes later (and it was now November 9) CBS announced that its computer

declared Kennedy to be ahead of Stevenson's 1956 vote in the industrial centers (by 12 percent), among the blacks (by 12 percent – an exceptionally high figure), in the suburban areas (by 8 percent), and in the farming communities (by 4 percent). The margin of the popular vote for Kennedy was now almost two million.

For the next two hours all seemed set for a Kennedy victory. But between two and three in the morning the lead Kennedy had built up began to narrow. The Midwest held the balance. Kennedy's lead in Illinois now looked far smaller. Kennedy was only six electoral votes away from the presidency. He found four in Montana, but in the South the Democrats had gone for independent candidates. Kennedy knew he had five out of the thirty-one electoral votes available. The other twenty-six were pledged to no one. It began to look as though the South would get its way, that the contest would have to go to the House of Representatives because neither Kennedy nor Nixon would have a majority. If that happened, it was a matter of "one state, one vote" and the South would then be able to make sure it got the candidate who would favor doing nothing very much about civil rights.

Sometime before four in the morning, Nixon went to bed, having refused to concede. JFK had also gone to bed and even though the Secret Service detail had begun to close in around the compound and one of the agents had said "Good night, Mr. President," Kennedy had by no means won yet. Robert Kennedy stayed in the communications center, telephoning endlessly. His brother could still win but only by the merest margin. The strategy had not worked as Robert had thought it would but the main thing was to win. Now even greater efforts were made to get the news in by telephone, and the bill for calls that night alone was more than $10,000. The Associated Press bulletins coming through between 5:00 and 6:00 A.M. announced that JFK had won in Michigan.

Opposite John F. Kennedy, 1960.
Below Kennedy sweeps to victory at the Democratic convention.

Hands reaching out to shake Kennedy's hand at the convention.

Now his total electoral votes stood at 285. It was enough to claim victory. When the first newspapers came on the streets their headlines were all saying KENNEDY. By 7:00 A.M. Kennedy had 50.71 percent of the overall popular vote. Nixon had achieved 49.29 percent. Later, in December, when all the votes had been counted the margin was even closer.

By December 17, 1960, Associated Press came out with their tabulation of the votes: Kennedy had won with 34,221,463 votes over Nixon's 34,108,582, with 502,773 votes going to other candidates. There was a recount in Hawaii while this AP record was being assembled. Originally, Nixon had been given 92,403 votes, and Kennedy 92,342 votes, but after the recount Kennedy came away with 92,410 and Nixon with 92,295. So, with this recount in mind Kennedy seems to have won by a margin of only 113,057 votes out of a total vote of 68,832,818. In fact, no one can agree on the final figures. Kennedy won by 111,803 votes, according to the *Congressional Quarterly*; by 112,801 according to the Republican National Committee's summary. Then the Clerk of the House of Representatives came out with another version. His margin for Kennedy was 119,450 out of a total vote of 68,836,385. Theodore H. White, in *The Making of the President 1960* complained fairly that, "Until the federal government sets up an official vote-counting agency these discrepancies will continue to baffle and annoy scholars and citizens alike." It is fair to say that John F. Kennedy became President, America's thirty-fifth, by a margin of not much more than .5 percent of the total vote.

Nixon was encouraged by Eisenhower to demand recounts in Illinois and Texas. Eisenhower even offered to set about raising funds to pay for it. "There is no doubt that there was substantial vote fraud in the 1960 election," said Nixon, who went on to call the Kennedys "the most ruthless group of political operators ever mobilized. . . . Kennedy's organization approached campaign dirty tricks with a roguish relish and carried them off with an insouciance that captivated many politicians and overcame the critical faculties of many reporters. . . . What if I demanded a recount and it turned out that despite the vote fraud Kennedy had still won? Charges of 'sore loser' would follow me through history and remove any possibility of a further political career. After considering these and many other factors, I made my decision and sent Kennedy a telegram conceding the election."

John Kennedy was now President-elect. Richard Nixon picked up the pieces of his campaign and went away to bide his time.

Chapter 3

President-elect

So we are all idealists. We are all visionaries. Let it not be said of this Atlantic generation that we left ideals and visions to the past, nor purpose and determination to our adversaries. We have come too far, we have sacrificed too much, to disdain the future now. And we shall ever remember what Goethe told us – that the "highest wisdom, the best that mankind ever knew" was the realization that "he only earns his freedom and existence who daily conquers them anew."
(John F. Kennedy, Assembly Hall of Paulskirche, Frankfurt, Germany, June 25, 1963)

Just before seven in the morning on November 9, 1960, the number of Secret Service agents detailed to protect the President-elect was increased to sixteen. They drove in a small fleet of cars from the Hyannis Holiday Motel at Hyannis Port to the Kennedy compound and surrounded it discreetly. They joined the small army of reporters and photographers who had waited outside the compound for most of the night. The Secret Service men had already been briefed to recognize the Kennedy family, their relations, and staff.

Opposite Hammer blows of the hand and a pointing or stabbing finger were two ways in which Kennedy would add emphasis to the points he was making.
Below On the day of victory, the family was photographed at Hyannis Port. *(Left to right, standing)* Ethel Kennedy, Stephen Smith, Jean Kennedy Smith, JFK, RFK, Patricia Kennedy Lawford, Sargent Shriver, Joan Kennedy, Peter Lawford. *(Left to right, seated)* Eunice Kennedy Shriver, Rose Kennedy, Joseph Kennedy, Jacqueline Kennedy, Edward Kennedy. November 9, 1960.

There are conflicting stories about who told Kennedy that he was to be America's next President. Maud Shaw, nanny to Caroline, records in her informal memoir, *White House Nannie*:

The new President was just a hump in the bedclothes, but Caroline shot across the room, jumped on the bed and pulled the blankets from her father's tousled head. He grunted, opened his eyes and smiled at his daughter.

Caroline played her part perfectly and with good timing.

She said nothing until he had given her a hug and a kiss.

"Good morning, Mr. President," she said, her eyes shining with delight.

"Well now, is that right?" Caroline looked over to where I stood in the doorway, and her father's glance followed hers.

"Am I in, Miss Shaw?" he asked.

He looked at his watch a bit doubtfully. "Well, I wasn't in the White House for sure at four-thirty this morning."

"Oh, I'm sure you've been elected, sir," I said.

According to Maud Shaw, JFK told her to check the results on the TV. But then, she tells us, she found that California was still to be decided. When the result came through, Kennedy simply said to her, "Well, there we are, then."

According to Theodore White, it was Sorensen, arriving at JFK's house at 9:30 A.M., who told Kennedy about California and that he

The three Kennedy brothers at Hyannis Port, 1960.

had won. Pierre Salinger arrived having already heard the news and while JFK had a bath, the three of them discussed the pattern of victory that had emerged during the dawn hours.

He breakfasted with Jacqueline and Caroline. After breakfast, Caroline was taken out by her cousin, Ann Gargan. An hour and a half or so afterwards, JFK appeared hand in hand with Caroline. She begged him to carry her piggyback style and the photographers encouraged him to do what his daughter wanted. After the photographers had taken their pictures, JFK invited his brother Edward, his sisters, Eunice, Jean and Pat, and Theodore Sorensen for a walk on the beach.

A neighbor called out, "Mr. President?"

Kennedy turned, amused.

"How do you like it?" the neighbor shouted across the fence.

"I don't know," Kennedy laughed.

Farther down the fence were some two dozen people who had come to the compound for an early look at the new President. A woman suggested they give a cheer but the cheer did not materialize.

Around eleven o'clock, JFK, Sorensen, and the Kennedy sisters returned to Robert Kennedy's house. There, on television, they watched Nixon's concession speech being read by his press secretary, Herb Klein. There was much banter among the Kennedys, and JFK compared Klein unfavorably with the

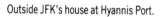

Outside JFK's house at Hyannis Port.

youthful, ebullient, cigar-smoking Salinger. Salinger recalls that someone in the Kennedy family said they thought Nixon might have had the style to appear in person. JFK replied, "He went out the way he came in – no class."

The only person who was not there was Jacqueline. She had gone for a walk by herself across the dunes to the beach. She was dressed in an old raincoat and sneakers, and wore a scarf around her hair, knotted beneath her chin.

JFK went off alone to find her and tell her the news. She had worked hard for him during the election, but even so, as Jean Kennedy Smith was reported as saying about Jacqueline, "I don't think she's mad about politics." Another friend had said, "It requires a more rugged, less feminine girl than Jackie to be vitally involved in politics." "She found it hard," wrote Arthur Schlesinger in *A Thousand Days*, "to get used to the ground rules." And Schlesinger later reflected:

The teeming world of the Kennedys was another problem. She had to fight to preserve her identity in this family of active parents-in-law, athletic, teasing brothers-in-law, energetic, competent sisters-in-law. There often seemed no point in trying to compete in politics, any more than in touch football; and she carried her self-defense to inordinate extremes, as when she would pretend a total ignorance about politics or impose a social ban on politicians.

Her mother-in-law, Rose Kennedy, put it slightly differently in her autobiography, *Times to Remember*:

We knew she [Jacqueline] had plenty of spunk and courage but we also knew she was rather a shy person who found a lot of public attention uncomfortable. She was not a natural-born campaigner.

Below Jacqueline had considerable misgivings about the life she would have to lead as First Lady. During the presidential years she made the role very much her own. **Opposite** Rose Kennedy, the President's mother, whose influence on her family both as matriarch and devout Catholic was constant and powerful. It was Rose, above all, who maintained the unity of the family during the years of private and public tragedy.

Jacqueline Kennedy, First Lady. This was the first official photograph taken in the White House, June 19, 1961.

At the same time, Jacqueline Kennedy, in spite of her shyness, her voice most often pitched at a scarcely audible whisper, was capable of defending her independence fiercely. A hint of this can be seen in her relationship with her father-in-law, Joseph Kennedy, whose biographer, David E. Koskoff, said of the Ambassador that he "admired her stout independence of personality and interests, and Jackie developed a great warmth for her father-in-law."

To start with, the warmth seems to have had a childishness about it: "According to her private secretary," Koskoff tells us, "Jackie and the Ambassador enjoyed a camaraderie in playfully seeing who could first hit a fleeing housekeeper with their lamb-chop bones."

That was sometime after Christmas in 1960. Later, after the Ambassador suffered his severe thrombosis in Palm Beach, it was above all Jacqueline along with Robert Kennedy, who tended him with selfless generosity.

Her new role, as First Lady, was of course determined by her husband and his office. It was to be more than ever political. Moreover, as First Lady, her position was publicly defined as secondary to JFK's as President. It became clear immediately that Jacqueline, young and independent, with good looks of a type not characteristically American, would define her role differently from that of previous First Ladies. Her husband was famous for being President, his own achievement. She was famous because she happened to be his wife. Worse, because, compared with Bess Truman or Mamie Eisenhower, she was "glamorous," she was exposed to an extraordinary glare of publicity. For her husband this was a great advantage. She was obviously a woman of style, who seemed to belong to his political New Frontier, but for Jacqueline it meant her life was no longer her own. Cocooned by bodyguards, her every movement a subject for gossip, her new life was not one she found easy to accept.

On his day of victory, JFK brought Jackie back from the beach below the family compound. The whole family had to change clothes for the photographers who took their pictures in the drawing room of Ambassador Kennedy's house. ("Ambassador

Jacqueline Kennedy wrote a weekly article, "Campaign Wife," for distribution by the Democratic National Committee. April 10, 1960.

The President-elect with his wife and parents.

Kennedy" was how the domestic staff and family friends frequently spoke of Joseph Kennedy even though he had not served as one for over twenty years.) After the photographic session, JFK was to face the press at the Hyannis Port Armory. The cars drew up to take the family and their associates on the short journey. Then there was a delay. JFK decided to overrule his father, who had insisted throughout the campaign on keeping out of sight. The old man knew his conservatism was out of tune with his son's image and was canny enough to know his presence could only damage his son's chances of becoming President. However, now that the campaigning was over and the election won, the son decided he wanted his father to appear with him in front of the world's press. JFK left the motorcade, and went back into the house, and persuaded his father to change into different clothes and join the family. Ten minutes later, with JFK in his white Lincoln Continental at the head of the procession, the family left for the Armory.

The family sat on the stage at the Armory. Jacqueline wore a purple coat and no hat, and looked very pregnant. Robert stood at one side of the stage beside the United States flag. Then, as his brother rose to speak, he moved away and sat next to his father who was withdrawn and brooding, his arms folded tightly across his chest. All fourteen Kennedys were there except for the President-elect's mentally retarded sister, Rosemary, who was in a nursing home in Wisconsin. JFK read out Eisenhower's and Nixon's congratulatory telegrams. He was asked what he was going to do next and told the press that he was preparing "for a new Administration and a new baby." Then the family left the Armory to applause. Surrounded closely by Secret Service men, they got into the four cars outside, and returned to the compound. Afterwards there was lunch for the whole family in Ambassador Kennedy's dining room. It was a typical, noisy, cheerful lunch. Someone pointed out that the Democrats had lost every state Edward had worked in. JFK repeated the story about Lyndon Johnson, who had telephoned the night before to say how sorry he was that ". . . *you* have lost Ohio. But *we*'re doing fine in Pennsylvania!" It was typical of Johnson to have been so self-assertive and typical of the Kennedys to find it so outrageously funny.

After lunch came a special Kennedy ritual: touch football. RFK's friend, Dave Hackett, established his "Rules for Visiting the Kennedys." Hackett, an old school friend from Milton, later became director of the President's Committee on Juvenile Delinquency and Youth Crime working with Robert Kennedy. Hackett's account of Kennedy touch football appeared in *The Saturday Evening Post* in an article by Harold H. Martin:

It's "touch," but it's murder. If you don't want to play, don't come. If you do come, play, or you'll be fed in the kitchen and no one will speak to you. Don't let the girls fool you. Even pregnant, they can make you look silly. If Harvard played touch, they'd be on the varsity. Above all, don't suggest

President Kennedy at his desk in the White House Oval Office, smoking one of the slim Cuban cigars specially imported for him from London.

any plays, even if you played quarterback at school. The Kennedys have the signal-calling department sewed up, and all of them have A-plus in leadership. If one of them makes a mistake, keep still. Run madly on every play and make a lot of noise. Don't appear to be having too much fun, though. They'll accuse you of not taking the game seriously enough. . . . Don't criticize the other team either. It's bound to be full of other Kennedys, too, and the Kennedys don't like that sort of thing.

. . . To be really popular you must show raw guts. To show raw guts, fall on your face now and then. Smash into the house once in a while going after a pass. Laugh off a twisted ankle or a big hole torn in your best suit. They like this. It shows you take the game as seriously as they do. But remember. Don't be too good. Let Jack run around you now and then. He's their boy.

Murray Kempton remembered the game that afternoon and the moment when someone knocked JFK down, and RFK, who had begun the move his brother failed to carry through, shouted above the din: "That's my brother – all guts and no brains." At the end of the game, it turned out that RFK's team had won.

The congratulatory telegrams were flooding in: a cautious note from Khrushchev and a grand one from England:

> ON THE OCCASION OF YOUR ELECTION TO YOUR OFFICE I SALUTE YOU. THE THOUGHTS AND SUPPORT OF THE FREE WORLD WILL BE WITH YOU IN THE CHALLENGING TASKS THAT LIE AHEAD.
>
> WINSTON S. CHURCHILL

JFK was in an ebullient mood at dinner that night, with Jackie and friends like Ben and Toni Bradlee, and William "Bill" Walton, the painter and a former journalist.

Ben Bradlee recalls that JFK greeted Toni Bradlee, who was pregnant like Jacqueline, with a big smile at Toni and Jackie: "Okay, girls, you can take out the pillows. We won."

They drank cocktails even though Kennedy at this stage drank very little and rarely smoked, except slim Cuban cigars imported discreetly from London. (Later, in the White House years, he drank rum daiquiris and especially liked such libation in the White House swimming pool.) This evening, with the Bradlees and Bill Walton, the conversation revolved around what to call the Chief Executive: Jack? Mr. President? Prez? JFK? Numero Uno? Kennedy said, according to Bradlee, that "Prez" would do for the time being. Later his friends only called him Jack when no one else was around. Otherwise, it was always "Mr. President." Bradlee also recalls in his *Conversations with Kennedy* a remark that Richard Nixon picked up with some glee in his autobiography some years later:

Over dinner he [JFK] told how he had called Chicago's Mayor Richard Daley while Illinois was hanging in the balance to ask how he was doing. "Mr. President," Kennedy quoted Daley as saying, "with a little bit of luck and the help of a few close friends, you're going to carry Illinois."

Nixon, of course, never said what Bradlee then adds:

Later, when Nixon was being urged to contest the 1960 election, I often wondered about that statement. I was told – by a member of the task force established by Nixon to decide whether or not to contest it – that the Republicans could well have stolen as many votes in southern Illinois as Daley might have stolen in Cook County.

Appointments were very much in everyone's minds. When dinner was over, JFK turned to Walton and Bradlee and asked if they could make one appointment each, what would it be?

Walton said that J. Edgar Hoover had been Director of the Federal Bureau of Investigation for thirty-six years and ought to be replaced. He did not offer an alternative name to Kennedy. Ben Bradlee spoke similarly about the head of the Central Intelligence Agency, Allen Dulles, another veteran who had been in the job for just over seven years.

Bradlee tells that he was in Robert Kennedy's house the next day within earshot of JFK. Lem Billings, an old school friend of JFK's, went to a telephone in the hall and asked the operator to get hold of both Hoover and Dulles. Bradlee recalls:

The next voice I heard was Kennedy's and he was telling J. Edgar Hoover how much he wanted him, was counting on him to stay on during the Kennedy administration. Laid it on a bit thick, I thought. A few minutes later, the whole scene was repeated with Allen Dulles. Thus ended my career as presidential consultant. Kennedy's offer, and Walton's and my suggestions, were made in jest, of course, but I never once recommended anyone to Kennedy after that, in or out of jest.

It is hard not to speculate how differently events might have turned out, had Dulles been immediately replaced. For one thing, the Bay of Pigs fiasco would probably have been avoided. It is also tempting to speculate as to why exactly Kennedy kept the two men on. Perhaps it was because the FBI Director entertained an intense dislike of the CIA, and the CIA, in turn, intensely disliked Hoover and his formidable bureaucracy. There was some comfort to be derived from two such organizations being possessed of so much suspicion of each other. Perhaps in Hoover's case he was privy to so much unpleasant or damaging gossip, so many half-truths, or, even facts about the Kennedys — especially the President-elect — that he had to be kept an ally.

J. Edgar Hoover was twenty-nine years old when he assumed the directorship of the Bureau of Investigation in 1924. Nine years later he personally renamed the formidable police bureaucracy the Federal Bureau of Investigation. A master bureaucrat, he also became a master of self-publicity. Pulp propaganda, from newspaper articles to movies, about Hoover's G-men and their heroics, swept across America. Immediately before the war, one commentator suggested that the FBI was "the greatest deposit of personal dirt ever amassed." Hoover's various obsessions included the FBI, horse racing, the pursuit of Communists, his mother, long hair,

The President-elect with his daughter, Caroline, and Mrs. Kennedy outside their home at Hyannis Port, November 9, 1960.

J. Edgar Hoover, Director of the Federal Bureau of Investigation, with JFK in the White House. Along with the Director of the Central Intelligence Agency, Allen Dulles, Hoover represented the old Washington power structure.

facial hair, red ties, damp hands, flies, germs and sex. William C. Sullivan, interviewed by Jack Nelson in the *Los Angeles Times* in 1973 described Hoover as a "master blackmailer." As soon as Hoover had evidence of a senator's or influential person's sexual or financial indiscretions, he would, according to Sullivan, let his prey know by saying, " 'We're in the course of an investigation and by chance happened to come upon this data on your daughter. Don't have concern – no one will ever learn about it.' Well, Jesus, what does that tell the Senator? From that time on the Senator's right in his pocket."

It was just possible that Hoover had nothing very much at all on the senator or his daughter, but few people in the public eye were inclined to call a bluff of this kind from the Director of the FBI. No one seemed entirely sure what was in the files, not even in those on the President-elect. But, eleven years after JFK's death, Jack Anderson wrote the following:

Raw FBI files, containing sensitive information about Presidents and other prominent people were sneaked out of the FBI after the death of J. Edgar Hoover.

The missing files, according to FBI sources, included reports on the sex exploits of the late President John F. Kennedy.

One report, for example, claims that in 1941 young John F. Kennedy romanced a woman suspected of espionage. His exploits with the lady occurred in Charleston, South Carolina, where he was working on a project for the Navy to protect defense factories against bombing.

The late FBI chief kept the files in his personal custody because he didn't want subordinates reading them and gossiping about their contents.

According to Joan and Clay Blair, Jr. the woman was one Inga Arvad, formerly a Danish Miss Europe, born on October 6, 1913.

She married an Egyptian, Kemal Abdel Nami, who later became Eygpt's ambassador to Paris. She divorced him, and after a short spell back in Copenhagen she went to Berlin, where she met Goebbels. She managed to get three exclusive interviews with Hitler ostensibly for the Copenhagen paper, *Berlingske Tidende*. She then traveled to America and went to the Columbia School of Journalism whose faculty were impressed by her journalistic achievements in Berlin. She moved to Washington and, through Arthur Krock, a friend of Joseph Kennedy, met Kathleen Kennedy and subsequently JFK. Inga Arvad wrote an article on JFK for the *Washington Times-Herald*. It was a shrill and unskilled piece of journalism:

The 24 years of Jack's existence on our planet have proved that here is really a boy with a future. . . . He is the best listener I have come across between Haparanda and Yokohama. Elder men like to hear his views, which are sound and astonishingly objective for so young a man.

That was just over a week before Pearl Harbor. Inga Arvad was now under the surveillance of the FBI; her bedroom was wired and JFK was one of several lovers. He called her Inga-Binga. This affair of JFK's must have excited and infuriated the prudish Hoover. Joan and Clay Blair spoke to Inga Arvad's son, who told them his mother and JFK went to see Hoover to complain about the surveillance. Hoover knew "she was *not* a Nazi spy or had ever been employed by the Nazis or did anything for them." But when JFK asked Hoover if he would be kind enough to produce a letter confirming that his girl friend was definitely not a Nazi spy, Hoover, Inga Arvad's son later told the Blairs, "said he couldn't because if he gave her a letter and then she went out and started working for them tomorrow his ass was on the line." Hoover presumably relished this request coming from the son of the former Ambassador to Britain.

Inga-Binga's contribution to this minor FBI melodrama of over forty years ago might well have remained just another item of personal dirt in Hoover's depository had JFK's career been less spectacular. Hoover, with his JFK file never far from hand, doubtless had his own view of the President's request that he remain Director. Of all Kennedy's appointments, J. Edgar Hoover, obsessive master bureaucrat, connoisseur of tittle-tattle, veteran law enforcer of another age, was by far the least characteristic member of JFK's New Frontier.

The rest of the evening of November 9, 1960, was spent at Ambassador Kennedy's house where movies were being shown. A John Wayne movie was put up on the screen and promptly booed off it. The replacement was *Butterfield 8*. Theodore White says the President-elect soon lost interest and walked out alone, no doubt to ponder on the problems he faced, now that the celebrations were all but over.

Chapter 4

Inaugural

We observe today not a victory of party but a celebration of freedom, symbolizing an end as well as a beginning, signifying renewal as well as change. For I have sworn before you and Almighty God the same solemn oath our forebears prescribed nearly a century and three-quarters ago.

The world is very different now. For man holds in his mortal hands the power to abolish all forms of human poverty and all forms of human life. And yet the same revolutionary belief for which our forebears fought is still at issue around the globe, the belief that the rights of man come not from the generosity of the state but from the hand of God.

We dare not forget today that we are the heirs of that first revolution. Let the word go forth from this time and place to friend and foe alike, that the torch has been passed to a new generation of Americans, born in this century, tempered by war, disciplined by a hard and bitter peace, proud of our ancient heritage, and unwilling to witness or permit the slow undoing of those human rights to which this nation has always been committed, and to which we are committed today at home and around the world.

Let every nation know, whether it wishes us well or ill, that we shall pay any price, bear any burden, meet any hardship, support any friend, oppose any foe to assure the survival and the success of liberty.

This much we pledge – and more.

To those old allies whose cultural and spiritual origins we share, we pledge the loyalty of faithful friends. United, there is little we cannot do in a host of cooperative ventures. Divided, there is little we can do, for we dare not meet a powerful challenge at odds and split asunder.

To those new states whom we welcome to the ranks of the free, we pledge our word that one form of colonial control shall not have passed away merely to be replaced by a far more iron tyranny. We shall not always expect to find them supporting our view. But we shall always hope to find them strongly supporting their own freedom, and to remember that, in the past, those who foolishly sought power by riding the back of the tiger ended up inside.

To those peoples in the huts and villages of half the globe struggling to break the bonds of mass misery, we pledge our best efforts to help them help themselves, for whatever period is required, not because the Communists may be doing it, not because we seek their votes, but because it is right. If a free society cannot help the many who are poor, it cannot save the few who are rich.

To our sister republics south of our border, we offer a special pledge: to convert our good words into good deeds, in a new alliance for progress, to assist free men and free governments in casting off the chains of poverty. But this peaceful revolution of hope cannot become the prey of hostile powers. Let all our neighbors know that we shall join with them to oppose aggression or subversion anywhere in the Americas. And let every other power know that this hemisphere intends to remain the master of its own house.

To that world assembly of sovereign states, the United Nations, our last best hope in an age where the instruments of war have far outpaced the instruments of peace, we renew our pledge of support: to prevent it from becoming merely a forum for invective, to strengthen its shield of the new and the weak and to enlarge the area in which its writ may run.

Finally, to those nations who would make themselves our adversary, we offer not a pledge but a request: that both sides begin anew the quest for peace, before the dark powers of destruction unleashed by science engulf all humanity in planned or accidental self-destruction.

We dare not tempt them with weakness. For only when our arms are sufficient beyond doubt can we be certain beyond doubt that they will never be employed.

But neither can two great and powerful groups of nations take comfort from our present course – both sides overburdened by the cost of modern weapons, both rightly alarmed by the steady spread of the deadly atom,

Kennedy takes the presidential oath at the Inaugural ceremony in Washington, January 20, 1961.

yet both racing to alter that uncertain balance of terror that stays the hand of mankind's final war.

So let us begin anew, remembering on both sides that civility is not a sign of weakness, and sincerity is always subject to proof. Let us never negotiate out of fear, but let us never fear to negotiate.

Let both sides explore what problems unite us instead of belaboring those problems which divide us.

Let both sides, for the first time, formulate serious and precise proposals for the inspection and control of arms, and bring the absolute power to destroy other nations under the absolute control of all nations.

Let both sides seek to invoke the wonders of science instead of its terrors. Together let us explore the stars, conquer the deserts, eradicate disease, tap the ocean depths and encourage the arts and commerce.

Let both sides unite to heed in all corners of the earth the command of Isaiah to "undo the heavy burdens . . . [and] let the oppressed go free."

And if a beachhead of cooperation may push back the jungles of suspicion, let both sides join in creating a new endeavor, not a new balance of power, but a new world of law, where the strong are just and the weak secure and the peace preserved.

All this will not be finished in the first one hundred days. Nor will it be finished in the first one thousand days, nor in the life of this Administration, nor even perhaps in our lifetime on this planet. But let us begin.

In your hands, my fellow citizens, more than mine, will rest the final success or failure of our course. Since this country was founded, each generation of Americans has been summoned to give testimony to its national loyalty. The graves of young Americans who answered the call to service surround the globe.

Now the trumpet summons us again – not as a call to bear arms, though arms we need; not as a call to battle, though embattled we are; but a call to bear the burden of a long twilight struggle year in and year out, "rejoicing in hope, patient in tribulation," a struggle against the common enemies of man: tyranny, poverty, disease and war itself.

Can we forge against these enemies a grand and global alliance, North and South, East and West, that can assure a more fruitful life for all mankind? Will you join in that historic effort?

In the long history of the world, only a few generations have been granted the role of defending freedom in its hour of maximum danger. I do not shrink from this responsibility; I welcome it. I do not believe that any of us would exchange places with any other people or any other generation. The energy, the faith, the devotion which we bring to this endeavor will light our country and all who serve it, and the glow from that fire can truly light the world.

And so, my fellow Americans: ask not what your country can do for you; ask what you can do for your country.

My fellow citizens of the world: ask not what America will do for you, but what together we can do for the freedom of man.

Finally, whether you are citizens of America or citizens of the world, ask of us here the same high standards of strength and sacrifice which we ask of you. With a good conscience our only sure reward, with history the

President Kennedy, the first American President to be born in the twentieth century, delivers the Inaugural address.

final judge of our deeds, let us go forth to lead the land we love, asking His blessing and His help, but knowing that here on earth God's work must truly be our own.

(John F. Kennedy's Inaugural Address, January 20, 1961)

For Joseph Kennedy, the seventy-one-year-old patriarch, his son's victory was a source of great delight. It was also a victory of investment and his calculated nurturing of old friendships, especially those with older journalists. No one can be sure how much money he spent on the promotion of his son's career. His huge financial resources relieved the Kennedy political organization of the burden of having to appeal for funds. Indeed, Kennedy's organizers never had to ask for financial help from supporters during the primaries, and the friendships made over the years, particularly with people from *Time, Life,* and *Newsweek,* ensured wide and favorable exposure.

But being a son of Joe Kennedy had disadvantages. The old man had a reputation for skirt-chasing, for doubtful financial dealing and the sort of crude behavior that snobs liked to say was typical of a man who had gone from an Irish slum to Harvard to an ambassadorship while making many millions on the way. Joseph

Above Joseph Kennedy; with his son at the Inaugural ceremony. During the campaign, Joseph Kennedy deliberately stayed in the background.
Right A draft of part of the Inaugural address in President Kennedy's own hand. These are the first phrases of Kennedy's famous appeal to the American people: ". . . ask what you can do for your country."

Kennedy had great charm, but it did not follow by any means that he was greatly liked. On the contrary, stories about the Ambassador's views on appeasement did not assist JFK in his pursuit of Jewish votes. But in the end the Jewish districts went chiefly to Kennedy and not to Nixon. In short, the Ambassador, money aside, was no asset even if he was not quite a political liability. He was asked about it to his face by Andrew Tully of *New York-World-Telegram and Sun* and the Ambassador replied:

"Let's not con ourselves. The only issue is whether a Catholic can be elected President."

It is hard to believe that self-effacement came easily to the old man. During the presidential years he rarely went to the White House. There may have been a mild streak of envy in the father's pride. Perhaps he was planning far ahead for the preservation of the political dynasty he had founded. In an interview on record in the

Kennedy Library, Charles Spalding remembered the father saying of JFK:

"I couldn't have done what he's done . . . I don't know how he did it. I don't know how he did it; I never could've done it."

Then he turned, and he said, "I'm like Bobby. That's the difference." And he said, "I don't understand that kid," pointing to the President in the pool, "I don't know how he did it."

It may be true that it was from his father that JFK inherited his sense of action, of the need to keep moving and get things done. He was impatient with compromise, like his father before him. Robert Kennedy said, after his brother's death:

President Kennedy was fond of quoting Dante, that "the hottest places in Hell are reserved for those who, in a time of great moral crisis, maintain their neutrality." If there is a lesson to be learned from his life and from his death, it is that in this world of ours, none of us can afford to be lookers-on, the critics standing on the sidelines.

But there would be many, subsequently, who would think that JFK, like his father, could well have thought more carefully about the likely consequences of some actions, particularly before authorizing the Bay of Pigs invasion and armed American involvement in Southeast Asia. But equally, on occasion he did not go far enough; for example, in civil rights and in social legislation generally JFK was initially hesitant. Indeed, it was James Meredith who finally precipitated the Kennedy brothers into taking an outwardly conspicuous and unequivocal stand on civil rights.

Left Joseph Kennedy with Rose Kennedy at the American Embassy in London on Independence Day, 1939. As the American Ambassador, Joseph Kennedy earned a reputation as a supporter of appeasement in those difficult days.
Right Ambassador Kennedy with JFK, boarding a plane at Croydon Airport, England, bound for Paris, March 10, 1939. JFK was twenty-two and this was his first trip to Europe.

President Kennedy's Cabinet takes the oath. *(Left to right)* Dean Rusk, Secretary of State; Douglas Dillon, Secretary of Treasury; Robert McNamara, Secretary of Defense; Robert Kennedy, Attorney General; J. Edward Day, Postmaster General; Stewart Lee Udall, Secretary of the Interior; JFK; LBJ; Adlai Stevenson, UN ambassador; Luther H. Hodges, Secretary of Commerce; Orville L. Freeman, Secretary of Agriculture; Arthur J. Goldberg, Secretary of Labor; Abraham Ribicoff (partly hidden), Secretary of Health, Education and Welfare; Earl Warren, Chief Justice of the Supreme Court. January 21, 1961.

On November 9, 1960, there were only seventy-two days until Inauguration Day. During this short time the President-elect had to form his Administration, make key Cabinet and policy appointments, facilitate the transition of power from Eisenhower and Nixon, plan for the Inaugural celebrations, write his Inaugural Address, consider the organization of Congress. All this when he was also very tired and wanted nothing so much as a holiday in Palm Beach.

First he selected his White House staff, those who would work most closely with him. Evelyn Lincoln, who had worked for him as his personal secretary for the past eight years at the Senate, continued in her job. Theodore Sorensen was appointed Special Counsel; Pierre Salinger was made Press Secretary. Kennedy preferred to designate his close aides "Special Assistants." Of these, Kenneth O'Donnell was in charge of appointments, a responsibility that sometimes brought him into minor conflict with Evelyn Lincoln; Larry O'Brien dealt with Congress. The other special assistants included Myer Feldman, Richard Goodwin, Ralph Dungan, and Arthur Schlesinger, Jr.. JFK's close friend Dave Powers was made "official greeter." A man gifted with an extraordinary memory for baseball facts and figures and stories of Massachusetts, he is reputed to have greeted Anastas Mikoyan with "Is this the real Mikoyan?" and the Shah of Iran with "You're our kind of Shah" – stories which hugely amused the President.

As for the Cabinet appointees, Kennedy told Schlesinger that State, Treasury, and Defense were giving him the most trouble. "I'd like to have some new faces here, but all I get is the same old

names. It's discouraging. But I suppose that it will take a little while to develop new talent." For Defense, Kennedy was encouraged to consider Robert McNamara, educated at the University of California and the Harvard Business School. McNamara had been appointed president of the Ford Motor Company the same week as JFK won the election. JFK sent his brother-in-law to Detroit with a brief to offer McNamara the post of Secretary of Treasury or Secretary of Defense. McNamara pointed out that he had only just started his new job at Ford. However, he agreed to go to Washington to talk the offer over personally with the President. Their meeting was a lively one. McNamara said that he really did not have enough experience to justify his appointment to such high office, whereupon the President said he had not had any experience with being President. McNamara accepted Defense. JFK appointed Douglas Dillon to the Treasury — a curious appointment insofar as Dillon had been Undersecretary of State in Eisenhower's administration. Dean Rusk, a Rhodes Scholar, former professor, and head of the Rockefeller Foundation, was appointed to State.

Two other problems now exercised the President-elect's mind. Who would run the Department of Justice as Attorney General and what job could he give his former campaign manager to whom he

Evelyn Lincoln, JFK's personal secretary. Mrs. Lincoln was the doyenne of the White House secretarial staff and Kennedy's invaluable aide.

White House Staff in October 1963. *(Left to right)* Kenneth O'Donnell, Pierre Salinger, Jerome Wiesner, Lawrence O'Brien, Kermit Gordon, Lee C. White, Timothy J. Reardon, Jr., Charles A. Horsky, Edward A. McDermott, Walter W. Heller, Ralph Dungan, Major General Chester Clifton, Theodore C. Sorensen, Richard Reuter, Bromley Smith, McGeorge Bundy.

owed so much, his thirty-four-year-old brother, Bobby? Kennedy had sounded out Adlai Stevenson for Attorney General. Stevenson had turned it down and let it be known that he was more interested in foreign affairs. He was duly appointed U.S. Ambassador to the United Nations. The name of Orville Freeman had been discussed, but in the end Freeman went to Agriculture.

RFK's view was that he did not want to work directly for his brother. So close a working association would not allow him space enough to pursue his own career, but he had little idea exactly what career to pursue other than possibly to run for election as Governor of Massachusetts. He turned down the suggestion that he might take his brother's seat in the Senate. In some ways the obvious thing was for Robert to become Attorney General, but Robert, like Stevenson, refused. His brother then mentioned the idea to a columnist from *The New York Times*. The paper commented adversely: Robert was too young and inexperienced for the job and JFK would be accused of nepotism. Nevertheless JFK decided to have Robert as Attorney General and, after considerable persuasion, Robert agreed to accept the appointment.

Benjamin Bradlee later recalled, in *Conversations with Kennedy* what happened next:

One sidewalk press conference that made all the history books but that never in fact occurred involved Kennedy's determination to name his brother Attorney General. When I learned it was in the offing, I asked Kennedy how he intended to make the sensitive announcement. "Well," he said, "I think I'll open the front door of the Georgetown house some morning about 2:00 A.M., look up and down the street, and if there's no one there, I'll whisper 'It's Bobby.'"

Robert Kennedy remembered that his brother told him:

. . . to go upstairs and comb my hair, to which I said it was the first time the President had ever told the Attorney General to comb his hair before they made an announcement. And then when we were outside he said, "Don't smile too much or they'll think we're happy about the appointment."

JFK made the announcement from the front of his house in Georgetown just before lunch on December 16, 1960. Of his brother, he said:

In looking for an Attorney General who must lead the fight for law enforcement, who must administer our laws without favor, and with matchless integrity, I have turned to a man in whom I have found these qualities. I have every confidence that he will bring to his new position this same ability, this same energy, this same courage, the same independence of judgment and this same integrity.

A reporter asked JFK if there was a precedent for a President appointing his brother to his Cabinet.

"No," the President-elect told his questioner. "We are going to start one."

Commentators had to search a long way back to find so young an Attorney General. Richard Bush turned out to have been one year younger, at thirty-three, when he was appointed in 1814.

JFK announces the appointment of RFK as Attorney General, outside his house in Georgetown.

Jacqueline and JFK at the first public appearance of John Kennedy, Jr., born November 25, 1960. The baby is wearing a forty-three-year-old baptismal gown in which JFK himself had been baptized.

On the afternoon of December 16, the two brothers flew in *Caroline,* JFK's own Convair, from Washington to Palm Beach with two of Robert's children, Joseph and Robert, Jr. Jacqueline was there with Caroline and her second child, John, who had been born by Cesarian section in Washington on November 25. The Georgetown house had been flooded with gifts for the new baby. Jacqueline's personal secretary, Mary Barelli Gallagher, had had the enormous job of sorting through every kind of bootee, romper suit, and blanket, and thousands of other presents.

In Palm Beach, at his father's house, JFK played golf, swam in the ocean, and relaxed. His swimming, beyond the high beach wall that surrounds the Kennedy Palm Beach house caused the Secret Service particular anxiety. And their clothing irritated the President. He asked O'Donnell to have them change out of suits and into more casual wear. It was during this period that he received a visit from Allen Dulles, head of the CIA.

Dulles came down to see the President-elect along with a man named Richard Bissell. They wanted to outline an intelligence initiative that Bissell had been planning for Cuba. The President-elect listened to Bissell carefully.

He heard that Eisenhower had approved the training of anti-Castro guerrillas. It was all costing some $13 million and the idea was to incite the Cubans to revolt against Castro. Bissell wanted Kennedy to allow him complete control over the adventure, which struck Kennedy as something akin to a World War II "special operation." To Kennedy, the plan was reminiscent of something out of a story by Ian Fleming, an author whose work he particularly enjoyed reading. Kennedy gave Bissell his permission to continue. Bissell asked that the Joint Chiefs of Staff not be told. The whole thing was to remain entirely clandestine — an intelligence operation, not a military one. The main thrust of the secret invasion that would launch this bit of derring-do was to take place at the Bahía de Cochinos – the Bay of Pigs – in Cuba.

Kennedy also worked on his Inauguration address. Theodore Sorensen, who was set to work reading all the previous addresses, recalls in his book *Kennedy*:

He wanted suggestions from everyone. He wanted it short. He wanted it focused on foreign policy. He did not want it to sound partisan, pessimistic or critical of his predecessor. . . . He wanted it to set a tone for the era about to begin.

Sorensen says of his reading of the past Inaugural addresses that he "discovered [them] to be a largely undistinguished lot, with some of the best eloquence emanating from some of our worst Presidents." JFK asked Sorensen to pay special attention to Lincoln's Gettysburg Address and Sorensen found that "Lincoln never used a two or three-syllable word where a one-syllable word would do, and never used two or three words where one word would do."

The pressure of meetings at Palm Beach and in Washington meant that the writing of the speech, JFK's most celebrated and

certainly one of the best known to be delivered in this century by any politician or world leader, did not start until January 13, 1961, only one week before he was to deliver it. A mass of suggestions for its contents came in from many quarters; some were asked for, some were not. Some came from Chester Bowles, Joseph Kraft, John Kenneth Galbraith, and Adlai Stevenson. Robert Kennedy made suggestions. Billy Graham sent in a list of lines JFK might use from the Bible. Sorensen approached the leader of the Jewish community in Washington for another list.

Sorensen, a superb speech writer, remains modest about the extent of his contribution to JFK's speeches. In *Kennedy*, he outlines how the drafts changed over the days before JFK delivered the final text:

First Draft	*Second Draft*	*Third Draft*
We celebrate today not a victory of party but the sacrament of democracy . . . And if the fruits of cooperation prove sweeter than the dregs of suspicion, let both sides join ultimately in creating a true world order – neither a Pax Americana, nor a Pax Russiana, nor even a balance of power – but a community of power.	We celebrate not a victory of party but a convention of freedom . . . And if a beachhead of cooperation can be made in the jungles of suspicion, let both sides join some day in creating, not a new balance of power, but a new world of law.	We observe today not a victory of party but a celebration of freedom . . . And if a beachhead of cooperation can push back the jungle of suspicion, let both sides join in creating a new endeavor, not a new balance of power, but a new world of law.

Harder-edged Anglo-Saxon words replaced the Latinate. More exciting, tougher nouns were brought in: "jungle" replaced "dregs," "beachhead" replaced "fruits," and so on.

It is odd that Kennedy left the writing of the final draft until so late. A hint at the reason for this may be found in Arthur Schlesinger's biography of Robert Kennedy. Schlesinger comments on Khrushchev's speech of January 6, 1961, in which he mentioned the triumph of Communism through Third World wars of "national liberation." This was the best way, Khrushchev declared, to bring "imperialism to heel." As centers of "revolutionary struggle against imperialism," Khrushchev picked out Algeria, Cuba, and Vietnam, and spoke similarly about Asia, Latin America, and Africa. In Washington it was thought the Russians were being more than usually belligerent. Schlesinger concludes that JFK read the Soviet speech as "a calculated personal test." So we find, in the Inaugural address:

Let every nation know, whether it wishes us well or ill, that we shall pay any price, bear any burden, meet any hardship, support any friend, oppose any foe to assure the survival and the success of liberty.

He specifically addressed his remarks to the "old allies," to the "new states," to "those peoples in the huts and villages of half the globe," to our sister republics south of the border. . . . *Let all our neighbors know that we shall join with them to oppose aggression or subversion anywhere in the Americas . . ."* These words were then tempered by:

Finally, to those nations who would make themselves our adversary, we offer not a pledge but a request: that both sides begin anew the quest for peace, before the dark powers of destruction unleashed by science engulf all humanity in planned or accidental self-destruction . . .

So let us begin anew, remembering on both sides that civility is not a sign of weakness, and sincerity is always subject to proof. Let us never negotiate out of fear, but let us never fear to negotiate.

Sorensen records JFK's remarks on the progress of the drafting:

The President-elect at one of the galas in Washington on the eve of his inauguration as President.

"Let's drop out the domestic stuff altogether. It's too long anyway. . . . I don't want people to think I'm a windbag. I'm sick of reading how we're planning another 'hundred days' of miracles and I'd like to know who on the staff is talking that up." [It has never yet been revealed who was. Perhaps the staff workers recalled JFK's own reaction to his election victory as "a miracle."]

"Let's eliminate all the 'I's. Just say what 'we' will do. You'll have to leave it in about the oath and the responsibility, but let's cut it everywhere else."

In the most famous of his remarks: "And so, my fellow Americans: ask not what your country can do for you; ask what you can do for your country" — "can do" was originally "will do." Only a few hours before he delivered his address JFK changed the "will" to "can." According to Arthur Schlesinger, the line was JFK's own, but had its genesis elsewhere. Kennedy had noted down Rousseau's remark, "As soon as any man says of the affairs of state, What does it matter to me? the state may be given up as lost." JFK had made similar remarks in his speech accepting the nomination of his party in 1960 and elsewhere. And, as Schlesinger points out, Justice Holmes had made a remark in his Memorial Day address of 1884: "It is now the moment when by common consent we pause to become conscious of our national life and to rejoice in it, to recall what our country has done for each of us, and to ask ourselves what we can do for our country in return."

Kennedy was also aware of his own speaking mannerisms and characteristics. His hands had a tendency to shake as he spoke in public, and though he enjoyed speaking, there was a great difference between the JFK who made witty remarks with an infectious, boyish smile to the press and the formal JFK who spoke to the large audience when the questions he put to his audience seemed studied and deliberate. Even the Inaugural was not free of this oratorical device:

Can we forge against these enemies a grand and global alliance, North and South, East and West, that can assure a more fruitful life for all mankind? Will you join in that historic effort?

A few people in the massive audience shyly called out "Yes" but the device was scarcely as successful as Kennedy had intended.

During the weeks around Christmas before Inauguration Day, January 20, 1961, which would be John Kennedy's day, the other members of the family were paid increasing attention by the press. *The New York Times* raised again the issue of Joe Kennedy's ambassadorship in London from 1937 to 1940:

Joseph Kennedy was said to have advised Washington not to aid Britain because Germany would win the war.

Although the President-elect had a majority of the Jewish vote, his father was accused of anti-Semitism. Reports by the German ambassador to London during World War II had indicated that Ambassador Kennedy "understood" the Nazi position on Jews.

The elder Kennedy protested that this was a lie. He pointed out that he was the only gentile member of a Jewish golf club in Palm Beach. But the charge hurt.

Now, in the same article of January 8, 1961, *The New York Times* concluded:

. . . the father is not seen as a tyrannical old man running the nation through an obedient son-President. As Joseph Patrick Kennedy grew more conservative through the years, John Fitzgerald Kennedy grew more liberal, until now, as the son has said, "our disagreement is total."

But the two men remain good friends. The Kennedy family solidarity has always been indestructible.

JFK was far from happy with all this press coverage, especially, according to Jacqueline's secretary, Mary Gallagher, of what Jacqueline was doing.

The Washington Daily News told that the First Lady was going to have the work of modern American artists on show in the White House. Jackie's newly arrived social secretary, Tish Baldrige, was asked how this could be achieved. What about the paintings already there?" "I'm sure it could be arranged," said Baldrige, "even if it means makeshift arrangements like hanging them in front of other paintings."

In order to see if the green paint in the White House dining room was covering up paneling, Jacqueline was reported as having said "I'll get my little knife out the first day and see what it looks like."

Carol Le Varn, also in the *Daily News*, said that Jacqueline described women's clubs receptions as being crowded with "those vast hordes of women" and then, apparently, corrected herself and called them ". . . those large groups of very interesting women." Then Betty Beale from the *Evening Star* brought up the question of Mamie Eisenhower. Why had not Jackie been invited by Mamie to have a look round her new home? Betty Beale was told the

Jacqueline Kennedy walks with her son, John, in the grounds of the White House.

invitation had not actually "been extended yet – but we hope it will be." There then appeared a banner headline next day:

JACKIE ISN'T DISTURBED ABOUT MISSING INVITATION

That was the last of the press conferences run by Jacqueline's Social Office.

Press comment on Robert's appointment was far sharper. "His experience," said *The New York Times*, "is insufficient to warrant his present appointment." The *Wall Street Journal* said the appointment was an "unqualified disaster." But the press attention wandered too wide across the Kennedy family and friends and the flood of new appointments for much of the criticism to stick. There was continuing interest in Caroline, in John Kennedy, Jr., and a brief diversion from such things when a man called Richard Pavlick went to Palm Beach with a car loaded with dynamite.

Pavlick waited outside the Kennedy house for JFK to leave to attend Mass. He prepared his explosives and pointed his car so he could ram JFK and blow himself and the President-elect to smithereens. When he saw JFK appear in the doorway with his wife and daughter, he changed his mind about the killing. It was not until three days later that the Secret Service arrested Pavlick in Palm Beach, as he was preparing to make a second attempt.

When he was searched a letter was found designed to be read after he had killed the President-elect. It read:

I believe that the Kennedys bought the presidency and the White House and until he really became President it was my intention to remove him in the only way it was available to me.

Pavlick was found to be insane. JFK wanted to know everything about Pavlick and ordered the protection of his family and himself to be tightened up.

Mamie Eisenhower at last invited Jacqueline to the White House to look over the mansion the new First Lady wanted to turn into a treasure house of American art and style. The tour was a brief one because Jackie had to leave a few hours later for Palm Beach. She went with two of her secretaries and was discouraged by what she saw. The bubbly Tish Baldrige made notes of the tour. The first point was spelled out with a liberal use of capital letters: "SHOCKING FACTS – The White House budget is TOO small."

The social intelligence report revealed that when the Eisenhowers held musicales their guests were given nothing at all to drink. "I just couldn't believe this!" Tish commented. She continued, in her note, published later by Mary Van Rensselaer Thayer:

SOS for Kennedy and Auchincloss knick-knacks. Every nice porcelain, silver or vermeil ashtray, cigarette box, table ornament, jardinière, cachepot, will be desperately needed. Please ask all relatives and friends to rifle their attics and basements for these goodies. Mrs. McC [Mary Jane McCaffree, Mamie Eisenhower's social secretary] said that for dinner parties there wasn't a nice thing to put down on the table in the way of nut cups, ashtrays, etc.

The White House was apparently being run without what the visitors described as "female taste (real)."

. . . in the State Dining Room, the only permanent plant or flower container on view for all the public, is a cheap $2.98 heavy white porcelain jardinière with 3 sick ivy plants in it, on the great marble mantelpiece.

It seemed that Ike and Mamie liked to dine off trays in their private sitting-room. The food had to be brought along corridors and passages and then up in the elevator through two floors. At the end of this journey it was invariably cold.

Various other items struck the women as odd. The swimming pool and movie theater had hardly been used at all. There was a small sunny room near an elevator shaft, that Ike had used as a painting studio. There was also a cupboard or what the visitors described as a "cranny" which contained a dental chair.

Tish Baldrige was impressed with the White House police staff. This body of men she described as "without doubt, such a fabulous, marvelous kind of creature . . . they alone are worth coming to the White House for."

They could hardly wait to start redecoration, but unfortunately tradition prohibited the new tenants from moving in until noon on Inauguration Day. But the resolute Tish Baldrige asked the Eisenhowers' social secretary if it might be possible to "smuggle a lot of stuff over without the Es knowing and she said, yes, the Head Usher could store cartons, suitcases, etc., out of sight and then whisk them into sight on the stroke of 12 noon. Isn't that marvelous??? Right out of Alfred Hitchcock."

As Mary Van Rensselaer Thayer concluded: "And so, a-tingle at the delicious prospect ahead, Tish signed off."

On January 20, 1961, at 12:51 P.M., John F. Kennedy was sworn in by Chief Justice Earl Warren. Before he took the oath, Lyndon Johnson took the oath as Vice-President. The Speaker of the House of Representatives, Sam Rayburn, administered the oath to LBJ. The ceremony took place at the Capitol's east front. Over seven inches of snow had fallen and the temperature was a raw twenty-two degrees. Gathered to hear the Inaugural address were more than twenty thousand people, and the police estimated that as many as one million others had turned out in the streets of Washington. During the three-hour Inaugural parade that he reviewed, JFK was bare-headed. Sometimes he would turn to drink hot coffee or chowder.

Marian Anderson sang "The Star-Spangled Banner," and Robert Frost, getting a few lines wrong here and there, read his poem "The Gift Outright."

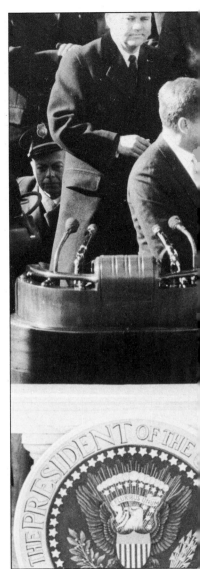

Above JFK with Richard Nixon, after the Inaugural ceremony, on the balcony of the Capitol.

Right The new President and Mrs. Kennedy, having returned to the White House after the Inauguration, walk to the reviewing stand to watch the parade.

Jacqueline wore a beige coat with a fur collar and a small pillbox hat and kept her hands warm in a mink muff. The invocation was spoken by Richard Cardinal Cushing who had officiated at her wedding ceremony. When he started to speak she genuflected. When her husband finished his address with the words "knowing that here on earth God's work must truly be our own," he acknowledged the applause and cheers and turned to look at his wife. As *The New York Times* reported next day, Jacqueline "gave him a 'you-did-all-right' smile" in return. When, later on, a reporter asked Mrs. Franklin D. Roosevelt how Jackie would manage the five inaugural balls that night, the veteran First Lady said, "I know she'll manage very well."

Then JFK went into the White House for the first time as Chief Executive.

At 10:00 P.M., in white tie and tails, he left to visit the Inaugural balls.

At 1:00 A.M., he said, "I think this is an ideal way to spend an evening and I hope that we can all meet here again tomorrow at 1:00 A.M. to do it all over again."

At another: "I don't know a better way to spend an evening – you looking at us and we looking at you."

Hardly anyone seemed to be dancing and even the orchestras and dance bands seemed drowned out by the political chatter, by the laying of ground for deals, and the feverish gossip and speculation about the new Administration.

JFK spoke at the fifth ball: "The Johnsons and I have been to five balls tonight, and we still have one unfulfilled ambition – and that is to see someone dance."

Jacqueline had gone home to rest. At 2:30 A.M. JFK went alone and mysteriously to the house of newspaper columnist Joseph Alsop. He had to wait several minutes on the doorstep for someone to answer the bell.

By 3:30 A.M. he was in the White House. He had issued an order that he wanted his staff at work next morning by 8:45 A.M. He would be the first into his office.

Opposite JFK at one of five Inaugural balls he attended in the evening of January 20, 1961.

Below The new President's first day in office. Now was Kennedy's opportunity to make real the phrase coined for his election campaign: the New Frontier. It implied a new approach to domestic policy, which can best be seen in Kennedy's struggle to make good his promise of equality for black citizens of the United States, and his decision "to go to the moon."

Chapter 5

The Bay of Pigs

I speak today in an hour of national peril and national opportunity. Before my term has ended, we shall have to test anew whether a nation organized and governed such as ours can endure. The outcome is by no means certain. The answers are by no means clear. All of us together – this Administration, this Congress, this nation – must forge those answers. . . .

The present state of the economy is disturbing. . . . Business bankruptcies have reached their highest level since the Great Depression . . . the American economy is in trouble.

A new housing program under a new Housing and Urban Affairs Department will be needed this year. . . . Federal grants for both higher and public school education can no longer be delayed. . . . Measures to provide health care for the aged under Social Security, and to increase the supply of both facilities and personnel, must be undertaken this year. . . . The denial of constitutional rights to some of our fellow Americans on account of race, at the ballot box and elsewhere, disturbs the national conscience, and subjects us to the charge of world opinion that our democracy is not equal to the high promise of our heritage. . . . But all these problems pale when placed beside those which confront us around the world. . . .

In Asia, the relentless pressures of the Chinese Communists menace the security of the entire area, from the borders of India and South Vietnam to the jungles of Laos, struggling to protect its newly won independence.

In Africa, the Congo has been brutally torn by civil strife, political unrest and public disorder. We shall continue to support the heroic efforts of the United Nations to restore peace and order. . . .

Below JFK with Secretary of State Dean Rusk at the Kennedys' Palm Beach home.

In Latin America, Communist agents seeking to exploit that region's peaceful revolution of hope have established a base on Cuba, only ninety miles from our shores. Our difference with Cuba is not over the people's drive for a better life. Our objection is to their domination by foreign and domestic tyrannies. Cuban social and economic reform should be encouraged. Questions of economic and trade policy can always be negotiated, but Communist domination in this hemisphere can never be negotiated. . . .

On the Presidential coat of arms, the American eagle holds in his right talon the olive branch, while in his left he holds a bundle of arrows. We intend to give equal attention to both. . . .

Dedicated men and women, not only on our college campuses but in every age group : . . have indicated their desire to contribute their skills, their efforts and a part of their lives to the fight for world order. We can mobilize this talent through the formation of a National Peace Corps, enlisting the services of all those with the desire and capacity to help foreign lands meet their urgent needs for trained personnel. . . .

I have asked the other governments concerned to agree to a reasonable delay in the talks on a nuclear test ban; and it is our intention to resume

Above President Kennedy receives a standing ovation just before delivering his State of the Union Address, January 30, 1961.

negotiations prepared to reach a final agreement with any nation that is equally willing to agree to an effective and enforceable treaty.

Let every public servant know, whether his post is high or low, that a man's rank and reputation in this Administration will be determined by the size of the job he does, and not by the size of his staff, his office or his budget. Let it be clear that this Administration recognizes the value of dissent and daring, that we greet healthy controversy as the hallmark of healthy change. Let the public service be a proud and lively career. And let every man and woman who works in any area of our national government, in any branch, at any level, be able to say with pride and with honor in future years: "I served the United States Government in that hour of our nation's need. . . ."

Our problems are critical. The tide is unfavorable. The news will be worse before it is better. And while hoping and working for the best, we should prepare ourselves now for the worst. . . .

Life in 1961 will not be easy. Wishing it, predicting it, even asking for it, will not make it so. There will be further setbacks before the tide is turned. But turn it we must. The hopes of all mankind rest upon us; not simply upon those of us in this chamber, but upon the peasant in Laos, the fisherman in Nigeria, the exile from Cuba, the spirit that moves every man and nation who shares our hopes for freedom and the future. And in the final analysis, they rest most of all upon the pride and perseverance of our fellow citizens of the great republic. . . .

JFK in the rocking chair that he used in the White House to ease recurrent bouts of pain at the base of his spine.

In the words of a great President, whose birthday we honor today, closing his final State of the Union message sixteen years ago: "We pray that we may be worthy of the unlimited opportunities that God has given us."
(from John F. Kennedy's first State of the Union message to Congress, January 30, 1961)

When we got into office, the thing that surprised me most was to find that things were just as bad as we'd been saying they were.
(John F. Kennedy, at a dinner in honor of his birthday, Washington, D.C., May 27, 1961)

JFK said at one press conference "This is a damned good job." The impression he gave to most people was that he was thoroughly enjoying himself. "John F. Kennedy," said Sorensen, "was a happy President." He brought an individual sense of style to the office and those around him responded with an extraordinary loyalty. He never held formal staff meetings with his special assistants, and very often they were sent off to report and compile advice, what the President called "options" – like "strategy" a favorite Kennedy word – without knowing that three of them had been given the same commission. He rarely said "Well done." He was not effusive with praise. He was meticulous in the choice of those he liked to work with and hated being alone. His close friend, Dave Powers, a man of resolute spirit and great humor, often stayed in the White House until the early hours talking with the President until he was tired out and just about to fall asleep. Kennedy rarely drank to

JFK makes the traditional opening day toss of the baseball season. According to *The New York Times* of April 16, 1961, "it is not known how President Kennedy's two ceremonial pitches last Monday rack up against those of his predecessors (starting with Taft in 1912). However, observers were sure they probably set a record — something like ninety feet."

JFK signs letters at his desk in the Oval Office while the Kennedy family friend, artist William Walton, hangs a painting by George Catlin. Also in the photograph is Mrs. Evelyn Lincoln, the President's secretary. This photograph was taken during the Kennedys' first few days in the White House.

excess. Only once, according to a close source, did he overdo it on champagne. He was an inordinately good listener. He endlessly questioned visitors, usually on their own special interests and personal expertise. he liked to learn how people mastered skills he himself did not possess. He disliked scatological jokes, but loved gossip and anecdote. Dave Powers was possessed of a limitless fund of the latter. Kennedy would ask him for a story. Powers would oblige, usually with some complicated piece of narrative from Irish Boston. The President would pause and, after a moment's hesitation, look away and laugh, most of all inwardly. He insisted, even after his election victory, on interviewing close employees himself. A former secretarial assistant recalls that she was actually given a shorthand and typing test by the President in person. He used a measure of foul language in private among his closest colleagues, though not with his family.

Certainly, John and Robert Kennedy took strength from their unusually close fraternal relationship. At times of political, national and international crisis JFK mainly relied upon his younger brother to raise his spirits. Another associate suggests that Robert was fonder of his older brother than the other way around. But insofar as Robert's devotion was complete this did not diminish JFK's affection for Robert.

Kennedy was plagued by recurrent pain in his spine, the result of football and war injuries, exacerbated, possibly, by a serious bone or gland disease. He had to have pain killing injections and wear a corset. His use of a rocking chair was intended less as folksy symbol than to ease the pain in his back. He also made full use of the White House swimming pool, and his associates and visitors would be invited to take a swim with him before lunch, though he was not a competitive swimmer. A hi-fi system was installed near the pool and he liked to listen to bland, undistinguished arrangements of well-known popular songs. He enjoyed golf more than he was prepared to admit but was not especially good at it. Playing a few holes, he liked to bet on each one with whoever was playing. He was as vain about his appearance as any politician, though an aide recalls that when he arrived at the White House, he looked "scrawny, hardly attractive at all." But, before the end of 1961, he put on weight and asked that items such as chocolate soufflés and other dishes that were sweet and fattening be cut out of the menus. He frequently worked without a jacket and tie on. But unlike his brother Robert he preferred not to be photographed without a tie.

He was perfectly capable of laughing at himself, and parodied his own Inaugural address at a dinner for the Democrats by saying, "If the Democratic Party cannot be helped by the many who are poor, it cannot be saved by the few who are rich." Sorensen records that Bobby Kennedy thought it "almost sacrilegious for him to parody his own solemn Inaugural."

In his book, *Profiles in Courage*, JFK began by describing courage as "that most admirable of human virtues. 'Grace under pressure,' Ernest Hemingway defined it." Sorensen recalled that

JFK laughed at that too by saying "it also described a girl he knew by that name."

He was usually awakened at the White House before 7:00 A.M. by his valet, George Thomas, who brought him newspapers and breakfast. As often as not, before taking a bath he would telephone Salinger or O'Donnell with comments on the latest newspaper editorials criticizing or commending the work of his administration. He was constantly on the telephone both from the Oval Office and from his private offices in the White House. Instructions were issued mostly on the telephone or through short memoranda dictated to Evelyn Lincoln, whom he called "Mrs. Lincoln," never "Evelyn." She bobbed in and out of the Oval Office like a yo-yo from her own small office just outside the President's door.

The Oval Office is twenty-eight feet four inches in width and thirty-five feet in length. From its high windows the President could look south through the winter trees to the Washington

JFK at his desk in the Oval Office surrounded by personal memorabilia. The scrambler buttons are clearly visible on the telephone console.

Monument. To the east the White House lawns and the rose garden could be reached by opening french windows.

Jacqueline arranged for a desk she had found in a White House room that Eisenhower had used as a broadcasting studio to be moved into the Oval Office. The desk was made from the timbers of HMS *Resolute* and had been presented to President Rutherford B. Hayes by Queen Victoria in 1878. It was the centerpiece of Jacqueline's scheme for the redecoration of the Oval Office. The theme was a naval one, comprising the desk, paintings of naval battles, and a model of the *Constitution* on the mantelpiece.

On the desk were personal mementoes: a glass ashtray with his Navy ID card encased in it, a coconut shell with the SOS message sent out when his boat was rammed by the Japanese during World War II off the Solomon Islands: "Native knows posit. He can pilot 11 alive need small boat, Kennedy" and a small plaque that read:

> O, GOD, THY SEA IS
> SO GREAT AND MY
> BOAT IS SO SMALL

Behind the desk stood the United States flag to one side and the presidential flag to the other. The three-inch-thick bullet proof glass in the windows muffled the sounds of Washington outside. The President used an eighteen-button telephone console placed on his desk. This, through the White House telephone exchange, linked him with the outside world. There were two other buttons on the console. One, colored red, activated a scrambler that enabled him to talk without fear of anyone being able to listen in or

JFK applauds Caroline's attempt to perform handstands in the Oval Office.

understand what was being said, provided that the person to whom he was speaking also had the necessary scrambler equipment. The red button also allowed him to cut into a call if the person he wished to speak to was on the line with someone else. Theodore White holds the view that "no President in recent memory . . . used his telephone more constantly, more directly, more intrusively in all the affairs of all his executive departments and bureaus than John F. Kennedy." On the telephone, JFK's manner was clipped and direct. He bothered with few informal pleasantries.

Once in his office, he read reports from the CIA and then prepared for the day's appointments and meetings which O'Donnell listed for him. He indicated when a meeting was over by getting to his feet – the sign that you were expected to leave.

Before the President had been in office a week, he was listening to advice that would lead him farther along the road to that disastrous adventure, the invasion of Cuba. Dulles and Bissell were very confident that such an assault could be a success. After all, six years before, the CIA had scored a success in toppling the Guatemalan government. Eisenhower had not hesitated to give *his* permission.

Kennedy eyed Dulles warily. He wanted more time to think about it.

The Joint Chiefs of Staff were asked for an assessment of the plan. They sent experts to look over the Cuban exiles training in Guatemala. The military seemed perfectly happy with all they saw. Kennedy obtained the opinions of his Cabinet and advisors. Only two were not in favor.

On April 10, therefore, the invasion force set off by sea from the Nicaraguan port of Puerto Cabezas. They were to take three key

Two members of the ill-fated force of exiled Cubans training in the Caribbean for the invasion of Cuba. April, 1961.

Training by American "advisors" did not prevent the actual invasion from becoming a shambles.

beaches in the Bahía de Cochinos. The CIA had planned, as a diversion to confuse Castro, another landing more than three hundred miles away from the Bay of Pigs. The CIA told Kennedy that once the invasion force landed they would be joined by thousands of anti-Castro guerrillas. Kennedy convinced himself that here was a Cuban force retaking their own country on behalf of the people. Two days later he gave a press conference in which he promised that no United States forces would intervene in Cuba:

. . . this government will do everything it possibly can – and I think it can meet its responsibilities – to make sure that there are no Americans involved in any action inside Cuba. . . .

The basic issue in Cuba is not one between the United States and Cuba. It is between the Cubans themselves.

This was, to say the least, disingenuous, since the invasion force of Cuban exiles was CIA-supported and funded. As it was, only a small proportion of the invasion force could have been described as trained fighting men. The majority were untrained civilians, some of whom were sixty years old, including three Catholic priests as well as doctors, lawyers, journalists, musicians and office workers.

Kennedy, sensing the possibility of failure, was told by the CIA that, in that unlikely event, the men would be able to escape to the hills. (What the CIA failed to tell the President was that the hills in question, the Escambray Mountains, were some eighty miles away from the beaches and to get there meant crossing swamps.)

The invasion force leaders had never been told what to do if the operation failed, which may well have been deliberate. After all, they knew their own country better than the CIA did and they would have realized the idea of retreat through the swamps to the Escambrays was hardly practical.

A preparatory bombing sortie by American bombers of World War II vintage, piloted by Cuban exiles, took place on April 15, forty-eight hours before the landing on the beaches. They flew over the Cuban airfields and claimed they had substantially destroyed Castro's air force. It was an exaggerated claim. Castro was left with quite enough aircraft to counter the sea attack on the Bay of Pigs. In any case, the ships of the invaders were ill-equipped and one of them, the key supply ship, had a damaged propeller.

In Washington, Kennedy was astonished to read accounts of the invasion in the newspapers. The CIA had employed a firm of public relations experts to incite the Cubans to counterrevolution. It could hardly have been a better warning to Castro to prepare his forces.

Aboard the landing craft, the invaders were in chaos. One of the pilots fell into the sea and his craft went around and around out of control. A machine gun went off by mistake, and before anyone could stop it, one man was killed and two were seriously injured. The CIA's clandestine radio station, Radio Swan, broadcast increasingly fatuous coded messages encouraging the resistance to rise up:

Alert! Alert! Look well at the rainbow. The first will rise soon. Chico is in the house. Visit him. The sky is blue. Place notice in tree. The tree is green and brown. The letters arrived well. The letters are white. The fish will not take much time to rise . . . .

In any case, none of the people who was supposed to take action in Cuba in support of the invaders ever actually heard the messages. Castro, alerted by the failed attack on the airfields, had at once rounded up more than two hundred men and women in Havana whom he suspected of being enemies of his regime.

When the invasion force reached the beaches, its members were astonished to see that, far from being the deserted place the CIA had thought it to be, it was in the process of being converted into a center for tourism. The final blow that effectively destroyed any hope the invaders had of landing as a coherent force was the discovery that the Bay of Pigs was scattered with coral reefs that would lacerate hands and feet.

At the United Nations, the Cuban Ambassador, Dr. Raúl Roa, accused the United States of naked aggression. His dignified protest began:

I should like to inform the Assembly, which is the supreme forum for the expression of the international conscience that this morning, at 6:30 A.M., United States aircraft . . .

At this point he was interrupted and told he was out of order. He then asked:

Which is of greater importance to the United Nations General Assembly, a purely procedural question or a breach of international peace?

The Soviet Ambassador chimed in, demanding that "the question of the aggression against Cuba" be debated. At the White House, Salinger was harried by reporters but refused to comment. The President kept up a normal routine of meetings and then went off to spend the weekend with his family at Glen Ora, the family's

Kennedy with former-President Eisenhower at their Camp David meeting during the Bay of Pigs crisis.

country retreat at Middleburg, Virginia. But the mask of normalcy was slipping.

Stevenson stood up in the UN and displayed a photograph of a plane bearing Cuban air force markings which he said proved that the bombing of Castro's air fields had been carried out by defectors from Cuba's own air force. In fact, though Stevenson was unaware of it, the photograph was a CIA fake.

On Sunday, April 16, Stevenson was told by Rusk that he had been duped. He wrote to Rusk:

No one will believe that the bombing attacks on Cuba from outside could have been organized without our complicity. . . . I do not understand how we could let such an attack take place two days before debate on Cuban issue in G.A. [General Assembly] Nor can I understand, if we could not prevent such outside attack from taking place at this time, why I could not have been warned and provided prepared material with which to defend U.S. . . .

After attending Mass, the President spent Sunday morning on the golf course with his brother-in-law Stephen Smith. He had to decide whether or not to let the invasion go ahead. Bissell had given him till noon to make up his mind, but in fact it was 1:45 P.M. when Kennedy told him to order the landing to be made.

Late on Sunday the exiles pressed toward the shore in their landing craft, following the guiding lights placed by the frogmen. (In spite of what Kennedy had said to the press, the frogmen were Americans.) The landing began around 2:30 A.M. on Monday, the worst time for a sea-to-land attack. Castro's air force succeeded in blowing up the supply vessels, destroying over three-quarters of the invaders' ammunition. Once on the beaches, the invading force found itself outnumbered almost three hundred to one. The fight was hopeless. Kennedy returned to a White House prepared to run a war, but throughout Monday and Tuesday the situation worsened. Salinger wanted to know what exactly to tell the press. Stevenson wanted to know what to tell the UN. There was secret talk of trying to rescue the fighters from the beach.

At 10:00 P.M. on Tuesday night, there was a congressional reception at the White House. Arm in arm with Jacqueline, the President appeared in white tie and tails smiling and relaxed as the band struck up "Mr. Wonderful." But just before midnight the President was called to the Oval Office.

For two and a half hours, still dressed in white tie and tails, the President, Lyndon Johnson, Robert McNamara and Dean Rusk discussed the situation with Admiral Burke and General Lemnitzer. Bissell, now unshaven and haggard, revealed to Kennedy the tragic details of the fate of the invasion force. Burke wanted to take in jets and shoot down Castro's planes, but the President refused to allow it. There was talk of sending in a destroyer, or unmarked planes, and of the exiles escaping to the mountains to become guerrillas. Bissell told the men in the Oval Office that plans for a retreat had never been given to the invaders. Finally, Kennedy

The President answers a question from United Press International's Merriman Smith, dean of the White House correspondents *(standing, left)*. It was Merriman Smith who later filed the UPI's reports of the assassination in Dallas. At this news conference, Kennedy was saying that it was not in the interests of the United States for him to comment on how much encouragement he had given the anti-Castro invasion forces. Seated beside the rostrum are Pierre Salinger, JFK's Press Secretary, and Andrew T. Hatcher, Salinger's assistant.

agreed to the dispatching of some B-26s from Nicaragua to give cover to the men on the beaches. He also agreed that six unmarked jets from the aircraft carrier *Essex* could, in their turn, cover the B-26s. The meeting broke up but the President stayed in his office talking to O'Donnell and Salinger till about 4:00 A.M. He was close to tears.

Even this last effort proved ludicrously ineffective. The two groups of planes failed to adjust their watches to allow for the different time zones. The bombers arrived on time at their target to find no jets other than Castro's, which shot them down. The whole episode, a resounding victory for Castro, had lasted only six days and Castro's forces captured 1,150 of the enemy. Bissell and Dulles resigned shortly afterwards.

At the height of the disaster, Tricia Nixon left her father a note by their hallway telephone.

JFK called. I knew it! It wouldn't be long before he would get into trouble and have to call on you for help.

Richard Nixon described his meeting with the President:

[Kennedy] jumped up from his chair and began pacing back and forth in front of his desk. His anger and frustration poured out in a profane barrage. . . . "I was assured by every son of a bitch I checked with – all the military experts and the CIA – that the plan would succeed. . . ." Everything had been going so well for him; a few days earlier he stood high in the polls, and his press overwhelmingly favorable. Now he was in deep trouble, and he felt that he was the innocent victim of bad advice from men whom he trusted. . . . It suddenly struck me how alone he must feel – how wronged yet how responsible. . . . [It] was not entirely his fault but nonetheless his inescapable responsibility.

Kennedy said at a press conference shortly afterward: "There's an old saying that victory has a hundred fathers and defeat is an orphan. I'm the responsible officer of the government." A press statement release emphasized what Richard Nixon had called the President's "inescapable responsibility":

President Kennedy has stated from the beginning that as President he bears sole responsibility. He has stated it on all occasions and restates it now. The President is strongly opposed to anyone within or without the administration attempting to shift the responsibility.

To Sorensen, he admitted:

How could I have been so far off base? All my life I've known better than to depend on the experts. How could I have been so stupid to let them go ahead?

It probably surprised Richard Nixon as much as it did Kennedy that early in May a Gallup Poll revealed Kennedy to be even more popular than ever. Eighty-two percent of the population supported the Administration. To Schlesinger and Mrs. Lincoln, JFK said, "It's just like Eisenhower. The worse I do, the more popular I get."

Chapter 6

Freedom Riders

This nation was founded by the men of many nations and backgrounds. It was founded on the principle that all men are created equal, and that the rights of every man are diminished when the rights of one man are threatened. . . .

It ought to be possible for American consumers of any color to receive equal service in places of public accommodation, such as hotels and restaurants and theaters and retail stores, without being forced to resort to demonstrations in the street. And it ought to be possible for American citizens of any color to register and to vote in a free election without interference or fear of reprisal. . . .

It ought to be possible, in short, for every American to enjoy the privileges of being American without regard to his race or color. In short, every American ought to have the right to be treated as he would wish to be treated, as one would wish his children to be treated. But this is not the case. . . .

We are confronted primarily with a moral issue. It is as old as the Scriptures and is as clear as the American Constitution.

The heart of the question is whether all Americans are to be afforded equal rights and equal opportunities, whether we are going to treat our fellow Americans as we want to be treated. If an American, because his skin is dark, cannot eat lunch in a restaurant open to the public, if he cannot send his children to the best public school available, if he cannot vote for the public officials who represent him, if, in short, he cannot enjoy the full and free life which all of us want — then who among us would be content to have the color of his skin changed and stand in his place? Who among us would then be content with the counsels of patience and delay?

One hundred years of delay have passed since President Lincoln freed the slaves, yet their heirs, their grandsons, are not fully free. They are not yet freed from the bonds of injustice; they are not yet freed from social and economic oppression. And this nation, for all its hopes and all its boasts, will not be fully free until all its citizens are free.

We preach freedom around the world, and we mean it. And we cherish our freedom here at home. But are we to say to the world, and, much more importantly, to each other that this is a land of the free except for the Negroes; that we have no second-class citizens except Negroes; that we have no class or caste system, no ghettos, no master race except with respect to the Negroes. . . .

It is not enough to pin the blame on others, to say this is a problem of one section of the country or another, or deplore the facts that we face. A great change is at hand, and our task, our obligation, is to make that revolution, that change, peaceful and constructive for all.

Those who do nothing are inviting shame as well as violence. Those who act boldly are recognizing right as well as reality.

"We preach freedom around the world, and we mean it. And we cherish our freedom here at home. But are we to say to the world, and, much more importantly, to each other that this is a land of the free except for the Negroes. . . ."

Next week I shall ask the Congress of the United States to act, to make a commitment it has not fully made in this century to the proposition that race has no place in American life or law. . . .

The old code of equity law under which we live commands for every wrong a remedy. But in too many communities, in too many parts of the country, wrongs are inflicted on Negro citizens for which there are no remedies in law. Unless the Congress acts, their only remedy is the street. (from John F. Kennedy's television address from the White House, Washington, D.C., June 11, 1963)

On May 6, 1961, the same week that Gallup gave his brother and his Administration the 82 percent vote of approval, Robert Kennedy traveled south to be present at the University of Georgia's Law Day. He intended to make his position on school desegregation perfectly clear. He had not always been a fighter for civil rights – as he told Arthur Schlesinger: "I won't say I stayed awake worrying about civil rights before I became Attorney General."

Harris Wofford, who was Special Assistant to the President for civil rights and a close associate of Dr. Martin Luther King, Jr., argues the case of a balanced view of the Kennedy brothers' commitment to civil rights in *Of Kennedys and Kings*. "It was late for a white man to be a President's Special Assistant for civil rights," Wofford recalls. He found himself "increasingly irritated by the patronizing attitude of many white liberals, who seemed to be moved primarily by a guilty conscience." Wofford remembers:

When asked to graph the rise of Robert Kennedy's civil rights consciousness after becoming Attorney General, Burke Marshall shot his arm straight up. My own graph would show something of a level line. . . .

One of the ties that I enjoyed with John Kennedy was a sense of the comedy of politics, but I began to think that the joshing might be letting him off too easily on civil rights. In any case, I got tired of his accosting me with a grin and asking, "Are your constituents happy?"

Harris Wofford considered Robert Kennedy to be the "vital center of action in civil rights." He recalls that the President "was prepared to sign the Executive Order on Housing over Thanksgiving in 1961 when he was having a rest with his family at Hyannis Port." Wofford wrote to JFK saying that once that was achieved he would prefer to work on the international front. But when the President came back after the holiday he told Wofford that the order "would be delayed again, at least until the spring primaries were over."

Civil rights, the granting of *genuine* equality and *genuine* rights, was very slow in coming. One of Kennedy's severest critics claims that Dr. King "exercised real power," that he "achieved changes that dwarf the moon shot as an American achievement. The 'Kennedy era' was really the age of Dr. King. The famous antitheses and alliterations of John Kennedy's rhetoric sound tinny now. But King's eloquence endures, drawn as it was from ancient sources – the Bible, spirituals, hymns, and folk songs. He was

Dr. Martin Luther King, Jr., addresses his followers including a child whose hands rest on the corner of his desk.

young at his death, younger than either Kennedy; but he had traveled farther." Against this can be set Wofford's account:

Martin Luther King, himself, came to see much more in Kennedy's "ability to respond to creative pressure" than mere political calculation and crisis-management. Kennedy "frankly acknowledged that he was responding to mass demands" but this was so, according to King, "because he thought it was right to do so." This is the secret of the deep affection he evoked. He was responsive, sensitive, humble before the people, and bold on their behalf.

It was the year of the Freedom Riders, but before they chose their moment, Robert Kennedy addressed the students in Georgia, his first public address as Attorney General:

I have come today to the great University of Georgia. . . . As students of the law of this nation you will know that it is my duty to preserve the law and make my solemn endorsement of the equality of each and every citizen of this land. . . . Do not imagine that all men in this nation agree, in their hearts, with you and me. But I do promise that we are maintaining the orders of the courts. We are doing nothing more or less. And if any one of you were in my position, you would do likewise, for it would be required by your oath of office. You might not want to do it, you might not like to do it, but you would do it. . . . Our position is clear. We are upholding the law. I say to you today that if the orders of the court are circumvented, the Department of Justice will act. We will not stand by or be aloof. *We will move.*

It sounded so very different from Eisenhower, who had said, "I don't believe you can change the hearts of men with laws and decisions." JFK had already appointed blacks to his staff – Andrew Hatcher, associate press secretary in the White House, and Robert L. Weaver, chairman of the Housing and Home Finance Agency. Kennedy had noticed no black cadets in the contingent from the Coast Guard Academy that marched in the Inauguration Day parade. The same afternoon he gave instructions for the admission of blacks to the Academy. But the actions of the Freedom Riders blazed brighter than did presidential appointments.

In May 1961, at Anniston, Alabama, a Greyhound bus carrying Freedom Riders was set on fire by angry whites. The Freedom Riders were testing segregation in Southern states, particularly at bus stations, where they planned to use restricted public facilities.

The congregation in the First Baptist Church, Montgomery, Alabama, waits for violence in the surrounding streets to die down. May 22, 1961.

The Freedom Riders challenged racism and segregation at lunch counters and rest rooms. In early May 1961, CORE (the Congress of Racial Equality) dispatched six whites and seven blacks on a bus going south from Washington. From Virginia they headed across the Carolinas, west to Alabama, through Mississippi, and on to New Orleans. The news of the violence that ensued staggered the Kennedy administration. Already humiliated by the tragic farce in Cuba and by the Soviets' successful orbit of the earth, Kennedy, preparing for talks with Khrushchev in Vienna, knew that racial violence at home would seem to show that his presidency was running out of control.

The white extremists were now alerted to the Freedom Riders' mission, and the worst of the violence started on U.S. 78. In Atlanta the Freedom Riders separated into two groups. One group boarded a Greyhound bus, the other a Trailways. They headed for Birmingham, Alabama. Six miles from Anniston, the Greyhound bus was ambushed by Ku Klux Klansmen who had armed themselves with a variety of clubs, sticks and chains. They intended to destroy the bus by fire, and succeeded. As the riders escaped the blaze they were systematically beaten up. Eventually the other group, traveling in the Trailways bus, heard what had happened and came to the scene of the attack to help those who were stranded and injured.

The Trailways bus was attacked in Anniston. Again there were savage beatings. In Birmingham, an even more vicious reception awaited the riders. Someone had told the FBI what was planned but the FBI did nothing. For half an hour a running battle took place in the Birmingham Trailways Terminal. The Police Commissioner, "Bull" Connor, told reporters that there were no police at the terminal because his policemen were off duty in observance of Mother's Day. The FBI had stood aside, filming the assaults. Not one arrest was made.

JFK sought out Wofford and asked him to have the Freedom Riders stop their journeying. Wofford told him that it was unlikely anybody could stop them now. John Seigenthaler, a close friend and assistant of Robert Kennedy's, was told to go and see if anything could be done. Seigenthaler flew straight to Alabama. A

Victims of police brutality in Birmingham, Alabama.

tall, resolute man from Tennessee who wore cowboy boots, Seigenthaler got assurances from Governor Patterson that the riders could and would be protected. The guarantee was tested next day when a group of riders boarded a Greyhound in Birmingham. But no one would drive the bus. Furious, Robert Kennedy spoke personally to the man in charge of Greyhound in Birmingham, George Cruit. Cruit recorded the conversation now in Robert Kennedy's papers at the Kennedy Library:

CRUIT: Drivers refuse to drive.
RFK: Do you know how to drive a bus?
CRUIT: No.

RFK: Well, surely someone in the damn bus company can drive a bus, can't they?. . . I think you should – had better be getting in touch with Mr. Greyhound or whoever Greyhound is and somebody better give us an answer to this question. I am – the government is – going to be very much upset if this group does not get to continue their trips. . . . Under the law they are entitled to transportation provided by Greyhound. . . . Somebody better get in the damn bus and get it going and get these people on their way. Mr. Cruit, I think that if some of your people would just sit down and think for a few minutes that somebody would be able to drive a bus 80 or 90 miles.

The bus left for Montgomery. At the Montgomery terminal angry racists were waiting. Again there were no police.

Seigenthaler arrived in his car to find that new violence had broken out. He saw a girl being attacked and went to her rescue. He was told to mind his own business. He struggled to get the girl away from her attackers and was pushing her into his car to escape when he was savagely hit across the back of his head. For more than twenty-five minutes he lay on the pavement unconscious, while FBI agents stood and watched.

When news reached Robert Kennedy that Seigenthaler had been wounded and was in the hospital, he was furious. Police Commissioner Sullivan of Montgomery was asked why an ambulance had

Opposite The passive resistance of one black demonstrator in Birmingham, Alabama, results in her being dragged into a police wagon.
Below Police used dogs and water hoses against demonstrators in Birmingham, Alabama. Eugene "Bull" Connor, the city police Commissioner was quoted as saying, "I want 'em to see the dogs work. Look at those niggers run."

On May 22, 1961, the congregation of the First Baptist Church was escorted to safety by U.S. marshals and local police. Violence had erupted around the church after Martin Luther King had preached there.

not been called for Seigenthaler. He replied, "Every white ambulance in town reports their vehicles have broken down."

Later, a federal court declared that the police department in Montgomery:

. . . wilfully and deliberately failed to take measures to ensure the safety of the students and to prevent unlawful acts of violence upon their persons.

Robert Kennedy telephoned Seigenthaler in the hospital to wish him well. Seigenthaler said, "You did what was right. Let me give you some advice. . . ."

"What's that?"

"Never run for Governor of Alabama. You couldn't get elected."

Law and order had broken down. To make the point and keep the peace, the Attorney General sent five hundred U.S. marshals to the area. When Dr. King went to Montgomery he was provided with an escort of fifty marshals, "just like he was the President of the United States," observed Governor Patterson with contempt.

Dr. King held a service at the First Baptist Church. Mobs of whites taunted him and other blacks at worship. The whites charged the lines of marshals throwing rocks and bottles. The marshals fired tear gas back. Some of the gas began to fill the church.

Patterson now called the Attorney General in a fury. Alabama, he insisted, was being invaded.

Coolly, the Attorney General inquired exactly who was "invading" Alabama. Patterson squared up to him and accused him outright of starting the trouble and violence.

"You can say that on television, John," Robert Kennedy said quietly. "You can tell that to the people of Alabama, but don't tell me that, John!"

James Meredith, aged twenty-nine, on his
way to attend his first class after enrolling
as the University of Mississippi's first black
student. The university campus was
guarded by 400 marshals and 1000 federal
troops. October, 1962.

"I'm telling you that. I'm telling you that the National Guard will protect the church successfully. I can't say the same for King."

"I don't believe you. Have General Graham call me. I want to hear a general of the United States Army say he can't protect Martin Luther King."

"You are destroying us. Destroying us – politically!"

"It's more important, John," RFK told Patterson, "it's more important that these people in the church survive physically than for us to survive politically."

The violence was temporarily contained, but not for long. The following year George Wallace took over the governorship of Alabama from Patterson.

In September 1962 James H. Meredith entered the University of Mississippi. The President spoke on television and told the people of Mississippi:

The eyes of the nation and all the world are upon you and upon all of us and the honor of your university and your state are in the balance.

Next day, *The New York Times*'s headline said:

NEGRO AT MISSISSIPPI U. AS BARNETT YIELDS:
3 DEAD IN CAMPUS RIOT, 6 MARSHALS SHOT
GUARDSMEN MOVE IN: KENNEDY MAKES PLEA

More blacks died as the violence continued. Kennedy pushed hard for his Civil Rights Bill, but it was not passed until after his death. Lyndon Johnson told Congress:

No memorial oration or eulogy could more eloquently honor President Kennedy's memory than the earliest possible passage of the Civil Rights Bill for which he fought so long.

Chapter 7

Jacqueline

George Bernard Shaw, speaking as an Irishman, summed up an approach to life. "Other peoples," he said, "see things and say 'Why?' But I dream things that never were, and I say, 'Why not?'"
(John F. Kennedy, addressing the joint session of the Dail and Seanad Eireann, Dublin, Eire, June 28, 1963)

Congress allowed the Kennedys $50,000 to do up the private rooms in the White House. A further $25,000 was provided to clean up and paint the exterior of the mansion. It was soon discovered that maintenance of the house had been somewhat neglected since it was last renovated, by President Truman, eight years before. So a further $100,000 was provided.

Jacqueline Kennedy called upon the services of her interior decorator in New York, Mrs. Henry Parish II. Mrs. Parish or Sister Parish as she is known brought in fabric samples, and within two hours the First Lady had made her choices. The former director of the National Gallery of Art, David Finlay, was asked to explain what the First Family could borrow in the way of paintings from the National Gallery and the Smithsonian. Jacqueline also discovered the hoard of furniture and domestic items that had been stored in the White House since Theodore Roosevelt's time. No catalogue of the hoard existed, so the First Lady went on what her colleagues called "spelunking" missions to see what could be rescued. Aubusson rugs were brought up from the basement. Marble busts were found in a men's lavatory. She discovered the *Resolute* desk that found its way into the Oval Office. Bellange chairs and a pier table were recovered from a government warehouse and restored. The First Lady commissioned the White House housekeeper, Mabel Walker, whose career had begun in FDR's time, to compile the first White House catalogue of all the items stored and on display. The rooms were also filled with floral arrangements, fires were lit in the fireplaces. Pale pink bedsheets were ordered for the Queen's Room, polka-dot linen sheets for other bedrooms. A system of "musts" were evolved. Mary Van Rensselaer Thayer describes the system:

The mechanical "musts" included checking to see that 18 bedrooms and 20 baths were tidied; 147 windows kept clean; 29 fireplaces laid ready for lighting; 412 doorknobs wiped clean; around 3,000 square feet of floor waxed, rewaxed, and often waxed again; half an acre of marble mopped and remopped; yards and yards of red carpeting vacuumed literally morning, noon and evening; 37 rooms dusted and redusted, some of them at least five times in 24 hours.

Sometimes the "musts" had to be seen to in the half hour between the departure of the day's last tourist (and a day could see between

Opposite above This family photograph was taken at Hyannis Port by the White House photographer Cecil Stoughton, and was a favorite of Jacqueline Kennedy's.
Opposite below The family celebrate Joseph P. Kennedy's seventy-fifth birthday in 1963.
Below The First Lady placing a candelabrum in the White House Blue Room.

fifteen and twenty-five thousand visitors) and the arrival of guests to a reception or dinner.

Seventy-four foreign leaders were guests at the White House during the first two years of the Kennedy administration. Special "cultural" events usually followed dinners. Grand Duchess Charlotte of Luxembourg was discovered to be a Shakespeare enthusiast so Basil Rathbone was called upon to come over from Hollywood and perform Henry V's St. Crispin's Day speech. The King of Morocco was given a shortened version of *Brigadoon*. The President of the Sudan saw an abbreviated version of *Macbeth*. Pablo Casals played after a dinner for the President of Puerto Rico. A dinner was given for forty-nine Nobel Prize winners and over a hundred other writers, scientists, and academics. JFK told them:

I think that this is the most extraordinary collection of human knowledge that has ever been gathered together at the White House – with the possible exception of when Thomas Jefferson dined alone.

The New York Times declared:

Command performances at the White House have become almost as sought after as those phenomena of political Americana, postmasterships.

From all over the country these days, the mail pours in: from glee clubs and prodigies, symphony orchestras and modern dancers.

Everyone, it seems, wants to get into the act with a one-night stand for President and Mrs. Kennedy and their guests.

Jacqueline's personal secretary, Mary Barelli Gallagher, found that her employer's personal expenses were causing JFK concern. During the second quarter of 1961, expenditures on clothing amounted to $35,000. A Givenchy bill came to more than $4,000. So an accountant was called in to regulate affairs. Even so, Mary Gallagher found herself taking "the long way around in the White

Left JFK thanks the cellist Pablo Casals after a performance at the White House on November 13, 1961.
Above The President and Mrs. Kennedy prepare to receive special guests at the White House. Jacqueline's poise and self-confidence as First Lady are clearly evident.

Above JFK, holding a small cigar, is offered what appears to be a dutiful reminder by the First Lady. May 11, 1962.
Right Robert Frost with the Kennedys at the White House after the dinner honoring Nobel Prize-winners in April, 1962.
(Seated, left to right) Lady Bird Johnson, Pearl S. Buck, the President, the First Lady, Robert Frost.

House halls to avoid meeting him [JFK]. I just couldn't stand the reproachful look on his face."

Various procedures for the regulation of what Mary Gallagher refers to as "their personal expenses" were devised. The First Lady's clothing budget was cut back, so too were "Food and Liquor" and "Miscellaneous" – that catch-all of household and personal items. The First Lady took her own stand on Food and Liquor especially Liquor. In her opinion, too much drink was being consumed at official functions. From now on (after November 1962), it was one guest – one drink. This restriction did not work however, when smaller parties were given at the White House and guests tended to wander off to look around. On such occasions the guests frequently put half-finished drinks down and walked about, only to find that the White House butlers had collected the unfinished drinks. Because no guest was to be abandoned without a drink, another would be offered. The First Lady's solution was noted by Mary Gallagher:

She [Jacqueline] instructed Anne [Lincoln, the new housekeeper] to tell the butlers to refill those glasses that looked relatively unfinished and didn't have lipstick marks on the edge. Jackie said to pass them around again – even if a few people got hepatitis.

Then came a day when the First Lady discovered trading stamps:

"Oh, Mary, do you know what I've just learned from Anne Lincoln?. . . You know, all the food we buy here at the White House? Well, she told me that with the stamps the stores give us, we can trade them in for these marvelous gifts!"

The First Lady's expenditures for the first year totaled $105,446.14. At the end of the second year they had increased to $121,461.61.

No First Lady in the history of the American presidency had excited as much controversy and public attention as Jacqueline Kennedy. Some have said that she was of no assistance to her husband because politics bored her, that she was possessed of a "splintered" or "fragmented" personality. Another view is offered by Gore Vidal: "Mrs. Kennedy, in particular, is a victim of the public's fickleness; undeserving of their love, she is equally undeserving of their dislike." She appeared distant and detached, rather as if she were above what was going on around her; she could seem defensive; and the characteristically low whisper of her voice, even during noisy conversation, drew her listeners quite literally closer to her. "I remember most," says Benjamin Bradlee in *Conversations with Kennedy:*

watching Jackie, and the almost physical discomfort she showed, as she walked slowly into this crowded hall to get stared at – not talked to, just simply stared at. Her reaction, later to become so familiar, was simply to

Jacqueline Kennedy photographed by Karsh of Ottawa.

pull some invisible shade down across her face, and cut out spiritually. She was physically present, but intellectually long gone. We were to see that expression a hundred times in the years to come.

In February 1971, Richard Nixon invited her, with her two children, to come to the White House to dinner and look at a singularly lifeless portrait of JFK. "Of course," Nixon says, "I was determined to keep the conversation away from anything that would distress her or make her visit sad. At one point she looked at me and said, 'I always live in a dream world.' "

It was the first time she had returned with her children to the White House after JFK's assassination, but Richard Nixon does not appear to have sensed her dislike of him.

Arthur Schlesinger's observation about her rings true. Her "greatest influence" on JFK was "to confirm his feelings about the importance of living his life according to the values he honored most."

In the White House: *(left to right)* Benjamin Bradlee, then chief of *Newsweek's* Washington bureau, Jacqueline Kennedy, Toni Bradlee, JFK.

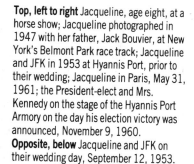

Top, left to right Jacqueline, age eight, at a horse show; Jacqueline photographed in 1947 with her father, Jack Bouvier, at New York's Belmont Park race track; Jacqueline and JFK in 1953 at Hyannis Port, prior to their wedding; Jacqueline in Paris, May 31, 1961; the President-elect and Mrs. Kennedy on the stage of the Hyannis Port Armory on the day his election victory was announced, November 9, 1960.
Opposite, below Jacqueline and JFK on their wedding day, September 12, 1953.

Jacqueline, Schlesinger recalls, once asked the wife of a politician:

"What have you been doing since the convention?" expecting her to say, "Oh dear, I've just been resting up since that madhouse" or something of the sort. Instead the reply came: "I've been writing letters to all those good people who were so helpful to my husband." "It was," Jackie said, "as if they were on television all the time."

Theodore Sorensen found that Jacqueline Kennedy:

. . . sensitive but strong-willed, so long as her husband would not be harmed by her decision, had no desire to be anyone else. By maintaining her own unique identity and provocative personality, she never bored or wearied the President. . . . As the Attorney General once commented, "Jack knows she'll never greet him with 'What's new in Laos?' " In addition, by continuing with her "fancy ways" and fox hunting, her water skiing and antique hunting, by refusing to appear more folksy at political rallies or less glamorous in poorer nations, by carrying her pursuit of quality and beauty into the White House decorations and dinners, she brought great pleasure to millions in every land, rich and poor alike.

Perhaps it was precisely because she found politics boring that she brought a wider dimension to JFK's life just as, however unacceptable it seemed to their critics, the Kennedys offered a new style in politics that captured, positively, people's imaginations at home and abroad. For a short while at least, a new breed of politician seemed to have taken over and, even if the takeover was not what many people wanted, political power had been gained by a new and younger generation. The First Lady was, above all, independent and, for better or worse, there have been no others like her since.

Chapter 8

To the Moon and Elsewhere

We choose to go to the moon. We choose to go to the moon in this decade, and do the other things, not because they are easy but because they are hard; because that goal will serve to organize and measure the best of our energies and skills; because that challenge is one that we are willing to accept, one we are unwilling to postpone, and one which we intend to win – and others, too. . . .

The growth of our science and education will be enriched by new knowledge of our universe and environment, by new techniques of learning and mapping and observation, by new tools and computers for industry, medicine, the home as well as the school. . . .

But if I were to say, my fellow citizens, that we shall send to the moon, 240,000 miles away from the control station in Houston, a giant rocket more than three hundred feet tall, the length of this football field, made of new metal alloys, some of which have not yet been invented, capable of standing heat and stresses several times more than have ever been experienced, fitted together with a precision better than the finest watch, carrying all the equipment needed for propulsion, guidance, control, communications, food and survival, on an untried mission, to an unknown celestial body, and then return it safely to earth, reentering the atmosphere at speeds of over 25,000 miles per hour, causing heat about half that of the temperature of the sun, almost as hot as it is here today, and do all this, and do it right, and do it first before this decade is out, then we must be bold . . . .

(from John F. Kennedy's speech at Rice University, Houston, Texas, September 12, 1962)

Opposite JFK addressing a crowd of 35,000 people at Rice University, Houston, Texas, September 12, 1962. "What was once the farthest outpost on the old frontier of the West will be the farthest outpost on the new frontier of science and space," said Kennedy about Houston.
Right The Astronaut John Glenn stands behind President Kennedy, who is looking into a space capsule.

J. Edgar Hoover dispatched a memorandum to the Attorney General with a copy to Kenneth O'Donnell, on February 27, 1962, to inform them that President Kennedy had had a relationship with Judith Campbell (later Mrs. Judith Campbell Exner). Between March 26, 1961, and March 22, 1962, seventy telephone conversations took place between Mrs. Exner in Palm Springs and Los Angeles and the President in the White House. The pattern of this relationship was revealed in some detail in leaks from the Senate Select Committee on Intelligence during November 1975 and first discussed in *The Washington Post* on November 16. It was also revealed that the FBI briefed its Director specifically about this relationship immediately before a meeting at the White House between the President and Hoover. The last call between Judith Campbell and the President took place on the same day, either before or after Hoover's visit at lunchtime.

Judith Campbell was introduced to JFK in February 1960 by Frank Sinatra. (Mrs. Lincoln was reported as having told the Senate Committee that she recalled Judith Campbell only as a worker for JFK during the California primary in 1960. It was her belief that they had not met since November 1960. Kenneth O'Donnell was said to have agreed with Mrs. Lincoln's view.) The relationship was additionally complicated by Judith Campbell's affair with Sam Giancana a few weeks after her introduction to the President. Judith Campbell claimed she continued her relationship with both men at the same time. The fever of the scandal heightened when it was revealed that Giancana and his colleague, John Rosselli, were together involved in a CIA plot to assassinate Fidel Castro. The plot was a pantomime enterprise. It involved the dispatch of Castro by poison to be administered by a lover of his who seemed to know he snored in his sleep with his mouth open and slept like a log. She was to pop a poisoned pill onto his tongue. The scheme never got off the ground at all. (Apart from anything else it was discovered the tablets containing botulism toxin would

Left The President with J. Edgar Hoover, Director of the Federal Bureau of Investigation, in October, 1962.
Right Judith Campbell Exner, who first met JFK in Las Vegas, during February 1960. After his death she claimed that her relationship with him had been "of a close personal nature" and had been free of "conspiratorial shenanigans."

not dissolve.) In 1975, during the summer, Giancana was shot dead while he was cooking sausages in his Chicago apartment. Almost a year later, the carved-up remnants of Rosselli were found in a seaborne oil drum off the coast of Miami. A year after that, Judith Campbell Exner published *My Story*. Fast on her heels came Kitty Kelley's *Jackie Oh!*, and the speculation about JFK's sexual encounters, technique, and manners seemed to sweep virtually any other consideration of his life and presidency aside. He slept, we were informed, with "countless women." There were "adventures in the presidential bed" and "nude swimming parties." A few names were named: Mary Meyer, sister-in-law of Benjamin Bradlee; Judith Campbell; Joan Lundberg Hitchcock, a friend of the Lawfords; Marilyn Monroe, who committed suicide. Mary Meyer was found murdered on the banks of the Potomac a few weeks after JFK's assassination.

Perhaps not since Kinsey has such excitement been generated by sexual statistics. But of the "countless women," the tawdry balance sheet of such putative confessions has yielded only a speculative and pointless number. Perhaps J. Edgar Hoover, prude and bureaucrat, enjoyed confirming his own suspicions. Norman Mailer has said that JFK "managed miracles of indiscretion." Maybe Hoover satisfied himself with the same conclusion.

"There is the old story," Hubert Humphrey once said, "about the mother who had two sons. One went to sea, and the other became Vice-President, and neither was ever heard of again."

It was hard to think up things to keep LBJ busy. It was equally hard for LBJ to accept a secondary role either in politics or in life. JFK appointed his Vice-President chairman of the Presidential Committee and made him chairman of the Space Council. Holding these two posts is alleged to have made Johnson remark characteristically when John Glenn was lifted into space, "If John Glenn were only a Negro!"

Dean Rusk said of Johnson during these years that he ". . .showed great self-discipline and strength. I think it was a major effort of self-control to fit into that role – with all that volcanic force that was part of his very being."

During the one thousand days of the Kennedy administration, Johnson traveled overseas to thirty-three different countries. Abroad, he was in his element. Arthur Schlesinger observed the following about the trips and Johnson's performance:

He sought his missions abroad, adored them and whirled through his thirty-three countries, scattering ballpoint pens, cigarette lighters, and general pandemonium in his wake and returning with trunks of gifts for his friends.

Johnson's great talent was for getting his way with Congress. But as Vice-President he was, in some senses, deprived of the relationship he had enjoyed in Congress; he was less effective than he could have been, partly because Kennedy was reluctant to use Johnson effectively in the one area where he could have been of greatest use. This was probably because JFK sought to direct his own program using O'Brien as his contact man.

Stories of Johnson's overseas travels amused everyone. His energy was seemingly limitless. The high point of the tour of India was Johnson's visit to the Taj Mahal. Here he gave Lady Bird a kiss, oblivious of the prohibition on kissing in the Taj. Then, to test out the echo, he gave a huge Texas yell. In Pakistan, on the way into Karachi, Johnson was enormously pleased to find the street packed with welcoming crowds. He ordered his motorcade to slow down so he could pump hands. His attention was caught by a man with a camel. LBJ strode up to him and asked the camel driver, "Why don't you visit the United States." The following morning the local papers were full of the invitation from LBJ to the camel driver whose name was Bashir Ahmad. They reported that LBJ had invited him to America, to stay at New York's Waldorf-Astoria.

When Johnson got back home, an assistant, George Reedy said:

He didn't think too much of it at the time but . . . we got an almost panicky cablegram from the American embassy in Pakistan, saying that this matter of Bashir Ahmad, the camel driver, had become a major *cause celèbre* in the country; and if, by God, Bashir the camel driver wasn't brought to the United States and put up in the Waldorf-Astoria, the Vice-President was going to look like the biggest four-flusher in history. So he kind of groaned and said, "Okay, bring him on."

A United States diplomat sought out Bashir in the heart of Karachi, only to find the camel driver had been spirited away by the police. They had decided they did not want Pakistan represented by Bashir in the U.S.A. But later, when Ayub Khan visited the United States,

Left Johnson extends both a hand and an invitation to Bashir Ahmad in Karachi on May 20, 1961.
Right Lyndon Johnson introduces Bashir Ahmad, in the fur cap, to a contestant in the livestock section of the Texas State Fair, Dallas, October 17, 1961.

Johnson taxed him about Bashir. LBJ wanted the little camel driver to see America, and eventually the diminutive Muslim's visit proved a successful public relations event. Even so, as one observer commented, it was a relief that out of the tens of thousands of people Johnson invited to Washington, only one ever turned up.

Johnson also visited Vietnam. Kennedy accepted the view of his military advisers that in Vietnam, the struggle for power there, as throughout most of Southeast Asia, would be carried out by guerrilla warfare. "Counterinsurgency techniques," the phrase of the time, would be employed against the Vietcong. This would be backed up by social, economic and political reform.

Johnson went to Vietnam with a brief to inspire Diem and assure him of American support. He was also told to do the same with the regimes in Thailand and Taiwan. LBJ got on famously with Ngo Dinh Diem. He called him "the Winston Churchill of Southeast Asia" and when he was questioned about this imprudent comparison by a *Saturday Evening Post* journalist, Johnson said "Shit, man – he's the only boy we got out there." Diem was in fact a verbose and narrow-minded president greatly under the spell of his brother Ngo Dinh Nhu and his sister-in-law Madame Nhu, who became known as the Dragon Lady. William Manchester wrote of two mysteries associated with the Vietnam War. Why did it become "a graveyard for the reputations of experts from the West . . .?" "Rarely in history," Manchester writes in *The Glory and the Dream,* "have so many eminent men been so singularly wrong about such an important event." And the second mystery Manchester pinpoints is ". . . why Americans of so many persuasions, including four Presidents, two Republican and two Democratic, felt obliged to rescue the Saigon government. The country was, after all, in Asia, five thousand miles away, a primitive land of rice paddies and dense jungle curled around the remote Indochinese peninsula. Yet for over a decade administrations in Washington battled desperately to keep questionable men in power in there, even at the risk of domestic tranquillity at home. The American effort in Vietnam was ill-starred from the outset. Kennedy should have seen that . . . he . . . fell under the spell of cold war rhetoric." His administration felt bound to "secure" Vietnam. But it was not bound to do so other than by general anti-Communist feeling which remained so virulent.

Kennedy was the first to dispatch the military, albeit for training missions. Diem's regime floundered. In May 1963, his soldiers fired on Buddhists celebrating Buddha's birthday. Eleven died. A month later, Quang Duc, a Buddhist monk, set fire to himself and was killed. This and other public suicides horrified the world. Kennedy was advised that the Diem regime must be removed. Kennedy changed his mind about an increase in economic aid to South Vietnam. The Nhus reacted furiously and attacked Kennedy, who did nothing, therefore, to prevent the coup which came on November 1, 1963. Diem tried to escape with his brother disguised as Catholic priests. He did not get far. They were shot and stabbed to death in Cholon. Madame Nhu blamed Kennedy. LBJ, friend of Diem, felt he had been betrayed. Just over three weeks later, JFK went to Dallas, and thereafter the course of the tragedy became the responsibility of President Johnson.

Kenneth O'Donnell recorded in *Johnny, We Hardly Knew Ye*, the memoir of JFK he wrote with Dave Powers and Joe McCarthy, that Kennedy said to his staff in 1963:

They keep telling me to send combat troops over there. That means sending draftees, along with volunteer regular Army advisors, into Vietnam. I'll never send draftees over there to fight.

Kennedy publicly reaffirmed this on television in an interview with Walter Cronkite on September 2, 1963:

It is their war. They are the ones who have to win it or lose it. We can help them. We can send them equipment. We can send our men out there as advisors. But, in the final analysis, it is their people and their government who have to win or lose this struggle. All we can do is help.

Perhaps he was saving withdrawal for his second term. If so, that was a policy the next President threw sharply into reverse.

On the other hand, if the exploration of space was a symbol of the continued struggle between the United States and the Soviet Union, Kennedy committed America to winning it with all possible speed and colossal expenditure. The cost of landing a man, an American, on the Moon was between fifty and sixty billion dollars.

JFK receiving a standing ovation at the UN in September 1963 after he had proposed a joint American-Soviet expedition to the moon.

He put out a feeler to the Soviet Union for cooperation in the venture on September 25, 1961 at the United Nations:

As we extend the rule of law on earth, so we must also extend it to man's new domain: outer space. All of us salute the brave cosmonauts of the Soviet Union. The new horizons of outer space must not be riven by the old bitter concepts of imperialism and sovereign claims. The cold reaches of the universe must not become the new arena of an even colder war.

To this end, we shall urge proposals extending the United Nations Charter to the limits of man's exploration in the universe, reserving outer space for peaceful use, prohibiting weapons of mass destruction in space or on celestial bodies, and opening the mysteries and benefits of space to every nation. We shall further propose cooperative efforts in weather prediction and eventually weather control. We shall propose, finally, a global system of communications satellites linking the whole world by telegraph, telephone, radio, and television. The day need not be far away when such a system will televise the proceeding of this body to every corner of the world for the benefit of peace.

Those who heard the President's appeal also knew that the Soviets were ahead of the Americans in space. It required no great act of the imagination to be persuaded that this also doubtless meant the Soviets were ahead in rocket research that would benefit their formidable arsenal of long-range missiles. Kennedy appealed in the spirit of the New Frontier; he had, the previous May, told Congress:

I believe that this nation should commit itself to achieving the goal, before this decade is out, of landing a man on the moon and returning him safely to earth. No single space project in this period will be more impressive to mankind, or more important for the long-range exploration of space; and none will be so difficult or expensive to accomplish. . . .

In a very real sense, it will not be one man going to the moon . . . it will be an entire nation. For all of us must work to put him there. . . .

No one can predict with certainty what the ultimate meaning will be of mastery of space.

I believe we should go to the moon.

It was a symbol in tune with the Kennedy of the New Frontier, and he left no one in any doubt that he wanted to be at the spearhead of the project that would convince the Soviet Union, and the world as well, that the United States was the undisputed champion and leader of scientific research and space exploration. It was a personal campaign, a campaign he almost always saw in terms of a political struggle. In spite of whatever cooperation he advocated at the United Nations, he saw the matter, as he said during his campaign, in personal terms:

The first living creatures to orbit the earth in space and return were dogs named Strelka and Belka, not Rover or Fido – or Checkers.

He had reminded his campaign audiences that Nixon had told

Khrushchev, "You may be ahead of us in rocket thrust but we are ahead of you in color television."

To which Kennedy replied:

I will take my television black and white. I want to be ahead in rocket thrust.

The Soviets pulled far ahead after the first lap of the race, when, on April 12, 1961, Yuri Gagarin, in the Soviet spacecraft *Vostok*, spent four and a half days in space.

Kennedy's promises sounded slightly hollow and he admitted to a press conference that he was tired. "No one is more tired than I am." He added that it would "take some time" to catch up with the Soviets. "We are, I hope, going to go in other areas where we can be first, and which will bring perhaps more long-range benefits to mankind. But we are behind."

There were frantic meetings between the President and his space advisors. Everyone agreed that something had to be done fast. American know-how was being exposed for not knowing how to launch a man into space.

The answer came almost three weeks later. *The New York Times* announced:

Above Kennedy with his scientific advisors in the White House in May 1961. To the President's left is Jerome B. Wiesner, his chief scientific advisor.

U.S. HURLS MAN 115 MILES INTO SPACE

SHEPARD WORKS CONTROLS IN CAPSULE

REPORTS BY RADIO IN 15-MINUTE FLIGHT

CAPE CANAVERAL, Fla., May 5 – A slim, cool Navy test pilot was rocketed 115 miles into space today.

Thirty-seven-year-old Comdr. Alan B. Shepard, Jr., thus became the first American space explorer.

Commander Shepard landed safely 302 miles out at sea 15 minutes after the launching. He was quickly lifted aboard a Marine Corps helicopter.

"Boy, what a ride," he said, as he was flown to the aircraft carrier *Lake Champlain* four miles away. . . .

The near-perfect flight represented the United States' first major step in the race to explore space with manned spacecraft.

This seemed to be the answer to Khrushchev who had heralded Gagarin as a Soviet version of Christopher Columbus only a few weeks before. The American flight was not actually anywhere near as impressive as the Soviets' had been but that was not the point for the moment. After all, America had gotten off the starting line and was now in the running. And for a while the disaster at the Bay of Pigs was forgotten.

A few months later, Captain Virgil I. Grissom was launched into space. The Soviets responded with Major G. S. Titov to which the Americans answered by launching a chimpanzee fed on tablets that tasted like bananas.

The deeply religious Colonel John H. Glenn, Jr. followed the chimpanzee on February 20, 1962, from Cape Canaveral, driven spaceward by an Atlas D rocket.

Right Watching the launching of the rocket carrying Astronaut Alan Shepard, 1961. **Below** JFK talking to John Glenn on the phone after the orbital space flight in 1962.

"Cape is go and I am go," the colonel radioed to earth in the spirit of Buck Rogers, who had been a boyhood hero of his.

Glenn came down safely, and LBJ greeted him with huge ebullience: "In my country we'd say you're pretty tall cotton. Were you very tense at takeoff?"

"I think I was," the colonel said, dazed.

"You were about as near the Lord's end as a person ever is," LBJ told the hero, philosophically.

The Presbyterian colonel smiled appreciatively.

The President was on the telephone by now.

"Listen, colonel," said JFK.

The colonel and the press listened.

"We are really proud of you."

"Thank you, sir."

"And I must say you did a wonderful job."

Then Kennedy hurried over from Palm Beach to Cape Canaveral to get in on the act.

In May 1962, Commander Scott Carpenter managed three orbits. But in August the Soviets rallied with simultaneous orbital flights by Major A. Nikolayev and Colonel Popovich. The exploits of Commander Walter M. Schirra, Jr., and Major L. Gordon Cooper followed, but the Russians answered with a woman, Junior Lieutenant V. Tereshkova.

JFK told everyone at Cape Canaveral they were doing a wonderful job, including Wernher von Braun, who had once advised Hitler on his rocket weapons. Von Braun became something of a national hero along with the other major space scientists and technicians. It was to be a long time before scientists would achieve such heroic status again. The comedian Mort Sahl said of Wernher von Braun, "He aimed for the stars . . . and often hit London."

On May 29, 1961, President Kennedy celebrated his birthday and made a speech in Boston, saying that he was going to meet Chairman Khrushchev in Vienna and at these discussions he would be "the leader of the greatest revolutionary country on earth." The next day, he was in New York where he said, "It is now one-thirty in Paris. I am due there at ten-thirty and I do not believe it would be a good start to keep the General waiting." Along with his wife, thirty-three members of his staff, and thirteen plane crew JFK left for Paris from New York's Idlewild.

In Paris, Kennedy met General de Gaulle for the first time. Unlike his wife, JFK did not speak French. He and de Gaulle had their talks alone, with their respective interpreters. They discussed the worsening tension in Berlin. De Gaulle advised Kennedy that the issues could only be resolved within a broader discussion of the easing of the Cold War and general disarmament. He encouraged Kennedy to be strong with Khrushchev. If the Chairman wanted to start a war over Berlin, then the West would respond. But it was de Gaulle's view, presumably backed up by secret intelligence briefings, that Khrushchev did not seek a war, especially not over Berlin.

The Kennedys lunched with de Gaulle. Jacqueline Kennedy and McGeorge Bundy spoke fluent French. They all got on surprisingly well.

The presidents later reviewed the position in Southeast Asia and de Gaulle outlined the difficulties the French had there. Then there followed a state banquet in the evening at the Elysée Palace. Everywhere the Kennedys went, the reception was cheerful and warmhearted. The interest of the French in Jacqueline was more than any of the presidential party had expected. Arthur Schlesinger described it as:

a good deal more than the instinctive French response to a charming woman. It had the air of a startled rediscovery of America as a new society, young and cosmopolitan and sophisticated, capable of aspiring to the leadership of the civilized peoples.

Above JFK and President de Gaulle in Paris, May 31, 1961.
Left On the second night of their visit, the Kennedys were entertained by de Gaulle at a brilliant dinner in the Hall of Mirrors at the Palace of Versailles. June 1, 1961.

Perhaps the French would not have conceded such leadership to the Americans or anyone else, but they conceded little in their admiration for Jacqueline Kennedy. There was another glittering banquet at Versailles in the Hall of Mirrors.

Before leaving Paris, JFK spoke at a press lunch, and declared,

"I am the man who accompanied Jacqueline Kennedy to Paris, and I have enjoyed it."

Air Force One landed in Vienna in the rain on June 3.

The first meeting with Khrushchev took place at the American Embassy that same morning. The two leaders disagreed about almost everything: Berlin, international control over nuclear testing, and a kaleidoscope of world issues. There was a grand dinner for all concerned at the Schönbrunn Palace where Khrushchev was asked by photographers to shake hands with JFK. He turned to Jacqueline, saying that he would rather shake hands with

Right Mrs. Kennedy with Premier Khrushchev at Schönbrunn Palace, Vienna, June 3, 1961.

her first. Later, JFK summed up his meetings by saying "No spectacular progress was either achieved or pretended."

In London the next day, Kennedy met Macmillan. The two men became close friends. Macmillan enjoyed Kennedy's humor. Each enjoyed the other's sense of mischief. Schlesinger said, "It was as if they had known each other all their lives." Even the formal photographs taken at Buckingham Palace when the President met the Queen looked informal and relaxed. The special relationship between the two countries seemed to mean more than it had for quite some time.

Left Kennedy and Khrushchev outside the U.S. Embassy in Vienna, June 3, 1961. **Above** President Kennedy and Prime Minister Macmillan. The strong friendship that existed between Harold Macmillan and JFK contributed greatly to cementing the "special relationship" between Great Britain and the United States.

JFK in the Oval Office speaking to the American people on his return from Europe, June 6, 1961.

Caroline Kennedy *(center)* bids farewell to her grandfather on the porch of his house in Hyannis Port.

The year 1961 ended sadly for the Kennedys. While playing golf at Palm Beach, Joseph Kennedy suffered a stroke. He was in his seventy-fourth year. JFK and RFK went immediately to Palm Beach. The stroke had left their father unable to speak. He could only make incomprehensible noises. The family visited him frequently, but there could be little hope for a recovery from the paralysis. Robert Kennedy swam with his father in the pool at Palm Beach, and was more than once reduced to tears at the sight of his father's condition. Benjamin Bradlee described a dinner at the White House:

Tonight was really quite unforgettable when Ambassador Joe turned up as a dinner guest at the White House with the Kennedys, Bobby and Teddy, Eunice Kennedy Shriver, Ann Gargan, and us.

The old man is bent all out of shape, his right side paralyzed from head to toe, unable to say anything but meaningless sounds and "no,no,no,no," over and over again. But the evening was movingly gay, because the old man's gallantry shows in his eyes and his crooked smile and the steel in his left hand. And because his children involve him in their every thought and action. They talk to him all the time. They ask him, "Don't you think so, Dad?" or "Isn't that right, Dad?" And before he has a chance to embarrass himself or the guests by not being able to answer, they are off on the next subject. Bobby and Teddy sang a little two-part harmony for him, after Bobby had suggested to Teddy, "Let's sing a little song for Dad." It was calculatedly bad and off key, but the ambassador leaned slightly forward in his wheelchair, tilting his head back to see them better, and was obviously delighted with their performance. For an encore, Teddy did his imitation of "Honey Fitz," bearing down on the false-tooth lisp, and everyone applauded, especially old Joe. Only he applauds with his eyes.

Chapter 9
The Cuban Missile Crisis

There has been a great deal of talk on the situation in Cuba in recent days both in the Communist camp and in our own, and I would like to take this opportunity to set the matter in perspective.

In the first place, it is Mr. Castro and his supporters who are in trouble. In the last year, his regime has been increasingly isolated from this hemisphere. His name no longer inspires the same fear or following in other Latin-American countries. He has been condemned by the OAS, excluded from the Inter-American Defense Board and kept out of the Free Trade Association. By his own monumental economic mismanagement, supplemented by our refusal to trade with him, his economy has crumbled, and his pledges for economic progress have been discarded, along with his pledges for political freedom. His industries are stagnating; his harvests are declining; his own followers are beginning to see that their revolution has been betrayed.

So it is not surprising that in a frantic effort to bolster his regime he should try to arouse the Cuban people by charges of an imminent American invasion, and commit himself still further to a Soviet takeover in the hope of preventing his own collapse. . . .
(from John F. Kennedy's news conference, White House, Washington, D.C., September 13, 1962)

Throughout the late summer of 1962, U.S. Navy intelligence sources reported a marked increase in sea traffic between the U.S.S.R. and Cuba. During August the CIA carefully studied intelligence reports from Cuban exiles and its own agents, and drew the conclusion that a massive and clandestine arms buildup was under way. Exactly how great it was, no one at that moment was entirely sure, except, of course, the Cuban and Soviet regimes. The convoys traveling west were carrying more than twenty thousand Soviet troops and technicians to service two dozen antiaircraft missile sites, forty-two bombers with nuclear strike capability, two dozen intermediaterange and forty-two mediumrange nuclear missiles. Khrushchev had timed the deployment of the force to coincide with the mid-term elections. So, with the Bay of Pigs still fresh in everyone's memory, Kennedy would have to face up to a Soviet nuclear arms deployment on his doorstep, which, as one commentator later concluded, would bring forward "Soviet attainment of nuclear parity by almost a decade." As Schlesinger commented:

With one roll of the nuclear dice, Khrushchev might redress the strategic imbalance, humiliate the Americans, rescue the Cubans, silence the Stalinists and the generals, confound the Chinese, and acquire a potent bargaining counter when he chose to replay Berlin. The risks seemed medium, the rewards colossal.

Castro and Khrushchev in 1960.

When the intelligence reports reached the Attorney General he commissioned a report to examine international law and advise him on courses of action he might recommend to the President. JFK learned that the transport of hostile weapons could be met legally with either a blockade or on-board inspections of the freighters. But obviously U.S. intelligence about the cargoes needed confirming. It seemed then extraordinarily unlikely that Khrushchev had embarked on so wild a scheme. Meanwhile, intelligence reports of military activity in Cuba were leaked to the Republicans, who promptly made the most of them.

JFK spoke at a news conference on September 13 by way of a reply to the Republicans. Cuba, he said,

. . . is under our most careful surveillance. But I will repeat the conclusion that I reported last week, that these new shipments do not constitute a serious threat to any other part of this hemisphere. . . . But let me make this clear once again: If at any time the Communist buildup in Cuba were to endanger or interfere with our security in any way, including our base at Guantánamo, our passage to the Panama Canal, our missile and space activities at Cape Canaveral, or the lives of American citizens in this country, or if Cuba should ever attempt to export its aggressive purposes by force or the threat of force against any nation in this hemisphere, or become an offensive military base of significant capacity for the Soviet Union, then this country will do whatever must be done to protect its own security and that of its allies. . . . We shall increase our surveillance of the whole Caribbean area. We shall neither initiate nor permit aggression in this hemisphere.

In spite of the force of this clear warning, it still seemed unbelievable that Khrushchev would make Castro a guardian of a substantial nuclear strike force intended solely to threaten the United States and bring the world to the edge of nuclear war. After all, Cuba was not a member of the Soviet bloc. It was thousands of miles away from the U.S.S.R. So it looked both politically and

Official photographic evidence of Soviet ships bound for Cuba.

OVIET SHIP POLTAVA ENROUTE TO CUBA

15 SEPTEMBER 1962

militarily unlikely that the Soviet Union could have embarked upon such a wild gamble. But, of course, that is exactly what it had done.

Spokesmen for the Kennedy administration insisted that if there was an arms buildup, it was not an *offensive* one. If there were Soviet weapons in Cuba, they were *defensive*. The Republicans disagreed about what constituted an "offensive" weapon.

Kennedy ordered more detailed surveillance of Cuba. It was a difficult undertaking. The spy plane pilots were understandably wary of the lethal Soviet surface-to-air missiles. Nevertheless, at the end of the second week in October, the U-2 pilots found what they were looking for.

The photographs they brought back showed the familiar pattern of missile sites, and on the morning of Tuesday, October 16 the photographs were shown to JFK by McGeorge Bundy, Special Assistant to the President for National Security Affairs. The President was having breakfast in his bedroom at the White House. He told Bundy to call a special meeting to begin at 11:45 A.M.

The meeting that took place in the White House Cabinet Room was the first of what became known as Ex-Comm: the Executive Committee of the National Security Council. The leading members of the team that determined the United States response to the U.S.S.R. during the thirteen day crisis were: The President, the Vice-President, the Attorney General, George Ball (State Department), McGeorge Bundy, Charles E. "Chip" Bohlen (newly appointed Ambassador to France and former U.S. Ambassador to the Soviet Union), General Marshall Carter (CIA), Kenneth O'Donnell (Special Assistant to the President), C. Douglas Dillon (Treasury), John McCloy (who had helped with the formation of the Arms Control and Disarmament Agency), Robert A. Lovett (formerly President Truman's Defense Secretary), Dean Acheson (former Secretary of State), Roswell Gilpatric (Deputy Defense Secretary), Robert McNamara (Defense Secretary), Dean Rusk (Secretary of State), General Maxwell Taylor (Chairman, Joint Chiefs of Staff), John A. McCone (Director, CIA), Theodore Sorensen (Special Assistant to the President), Edwin M. Martin (Assistant Secretary of State for Latin America), Llewellyn Thompson (former U.S. Ambassador to the Soviet Union), and Adlai Stevenson (U.S. Ambassador to the United Nations). This committee bore the hallmark of Kennedy's administrative style. Its members were trusted advisors. Three of them — Acheson, Lovett and McCloy — were private citizens but possessed considerable experience in government. Ex-Comm was not the same thing as the much larger National Security Council. Kennedy did not like formal meetings, especially Cabinet meetings. Ex-Comm would be free of tiresome procedures.

It received the first revealing intelligence reports with what JFK described as "shocked incredulity." The missile site built at San Cristóbal would be operational in less than two weeks. After that the United States could only get between two and three minutes warning of a nuclear strike.

The President immediately ordered more U-2 flights over Cuba, irrespective of the risks of attack by the SAMs. He instructed Rusk to make secret inquiries among America's allies in Latin America and Europe and to assess the extent of the support they could expect, and McNamara was told to review military capabilities.

When the discussion became more general, it was agreed that a sudden and dramatic response would make matters worse; on the other hand, something had to be done. Obviously, no one thought Khrushchev should be allowed a free hand to do what he liked. Preventative or retaliatory action was needed. The question was — what sort?

The President presides over a top-secret meeting of the National Security Council, April 27, 1962. The President is flanked on his right by Dean Rusk and on his left by Robert McNamara. The Attorney General, Robert Kennedy, is just visible at the far end of the room with his hand to his face.

As the meeting broke up Kennedy told everyone in the Cabinet Room to say absolutely nothing about the discussions. There was to be no mention made of these events to families or staffs.

In the afternoon Kennedy had a meeting with Stevenson, who advocated finding a peaceful solution at all costs. Stevenson encouraged JFK to keep to his schedule of political campaigning that was about to start, and Kennedy accepted the idea of letting everyone believe it was business as usual.

Fay Kohler, U.S. Ambassador in Moscow, was summoned that same day by Khrushchev, whom the Ambassador found to be in high spirits after a holiday on the Black Sea coast. Khrushchev wanted Kohler to tell the President that Soviet equipment and personnel in Cuba were there for entirely defensive purposes. Khrushchev said he was sorry to learn that there had been misunderstandings that might embarrass the President so near the midterm elections. His evasion and that of the Soviet Ambassador in Washington, Anatoly Dobrynin, convinced no one. Later, however, Robert Kennedy said that he believed Dobrynin had not been fully informed. Perhaps Dobrynin did not lie to him; he simply did not then know what was going on.

By the end of October 16, the opinion of Ex-Comm seemed to be leaning toward an air strike. RFK wrote a few words and passed them to the President. They read: *I now know how Tojo felt when he was planning Pearl Harbor.*

Further grim intelligence was received the next day by Ex-Comm, which met in George Ball's conference room in the State Department. The Soviets had begun placing mediumrange ballistic missiles with a range of 1,000 miles and intermediaterange

A greatly enlarged photograph of mediumrange ballistic missile launch site number 3, San Cristóbal, Cuba, October 29, 1962.

missiles capable of hitting targets 2,200 miles away. These were being set up at San Cristóbal and Guanajay, and from there it was clear the Soviets could hit American targets as far off as Montana and Wyoming, with forty nuclear warheads.

The President was absent from the day's meetings on Wednesday October 17. He had gone to Connecticut to speak on behalf of his long-time supporter, Abraham Ribicoff, who was running for the Senate. In his absence, chairmanship of the meeting would have fallen to Dean Rusk, the senior member of the Cabinet in Ex-Comm, but in fact it was Robert Kennedy who led the discussion.

Six options or, as they were called, "tracks" were put up for discussion:

Track A: Do nothing.
Track B: Send an emissary to Khrushchev and demand removal.
Track C: Call the U.S.S.R. and Cuba before the UN Security Council. (This was rejected because the Soviet UN Ambassador happened to be the present chairman of the Security Council. Anyway, the Soviet Union had a veto.)
Track D: Blockade.
Track E: Air strike.
Track F: Invasion.

George Ball spoke out against the air strike. It was not in the American spirit to launch surprise attacks. Robert agreed with him and spoke about Pearl Harbor. Why should his brother be the Tojo of the 1960s?

This was too much for the sixty-nine-year-old former Secretary of State, Dean Acheson. The warrior of the Cold War spoke

San Cristóbal, Cuba. Further evidence of the Soviet presence.

contemptuously of Bobby Kennedy's analogy of Pearl Harbor with the present situation. Robert Kennedy spoke of the moral issue. Why should America be held responsible for the loss of thousands of innocent Cuban lives? Irritated and fed up with the discussion of the moral issue, Acheson said that the President already had the power vested in him by Congress to stop the arms buildup ". . . *by whatever means may be necessary, including the use of arms.*"

The President came back to Washington at midnight. He learned that the Soviet missiles in Cuba were now sited so that they could pick off densely populated areas within the United States and that the strike force constituted 50 percent of the Soviet Union's arsenal of intercontinental ballistic missiles. It would take less than five minutes for between seventy and ninety million Americans to be slaughtered once Khrushchev gave the command to fire.

The next morning he called Dean Acheson over to the White House and spoke of the Pearl Harbor analogy. Acheson dismissed what he described as Bobby Kennedy's emotional approach. It was "silly," "a cliché," and "unworthy." The President showed Acheson the door, telling him, "This is the week when I had better earn my salary."

Throughout Thursday the discussion continued in secret, and Ex-Comm was beginning to divide into two distinct groups, becoming either hawks or doves – words which would soon become part of the 1960s war jargon.

McNamara was for blockade, as was Robert Kennedy. In the morning, Rusk was against a surprise attack; in the afternoon, he changed his mind. McGeorge Bundy also changed his views and then changed them back again. Kennedy led the discussion towards longer-term aims; maybe they should go the whole way and get rid of Castro once and for all? But the Bay of Pigs was never far from Kennedy's mind and such ideas were cast aside. Sometimes Kennedy would deliberately stay away from the discussions to allow Ex-Comm freer rein to unravel the problems. At five o'clock, Andrei Gromyko, the Soviet Foreign Minister, kept a long-standing appointment with Kennedy at the White House. Their talk first turned to Germany and Berlin, then to Cuba. Gromyko told Kennedy that he could not understand why the United States felt so threatened by a "baby" nation like Cuba. Kennedy insisted that the presence of Soviet arms there was indeed a threat. Gromyko countered with a reminder of the Bay of Pigs. Kennedy interrupted him and said he had already admitted to Khrushchev in Vienna that the operation had been an error. He went on to remind Gromyko that he had said, very clearly, that the United States would not tolerate an aggressive Soviet presence in Cuba, so close to America's shores. He also told Gromyko that as President he had told the American people that the Soviet presence in Cuba constituted a program of military assistance. In essence, it was defensive. But, said Kennedy, if that were to change, it would have the most serious implications for world peace. He thus gave Gromyko every opportunity to admit to the presence of the

JFK with Andrei Gromyko, Soviet Minister of Foreign Affairs, in the Oval Office, March 27, 1961.

missiles. Gromyko made no such admission and left the White House, cheerfully telling newsmen that his meeting with the President had been "useful, most useful."'

Kennedy had avoided telling Gromyko what *he* knew simply because he had not yet, by any means, made up his mind what he was going to do. That evening Dean Rusk hosted a dinner for Gromyko at the State Department. The formal joviality took place in the State Department's dining room on the eighth floor. One floor below, in George Ball's office, Ex-Comm members talked on relentlessly. At one point, some newsmen were surprised to see McNamara and McCone get out of the elevator on the eighth. They could not understand why the Secretary of Defense and the head of the CIA were going to dinner with Gromyko. In an encounter of delightful farce, McNamara, smiling broadly at the reporters, said, "Yes – we're joining the party," and stepped back into the elevator. They had pressed the wrong button and gone to the wrong floor. Down they went to the right floor and hurried into the secret meeting in Ball's office.

The hawks and doves were taking sides more decisively. Ball, RFK, McNamara, Gilpatric, Lovett, and Thompson were doves, arguing for the blockade; Acheson, Bundy, Dillon, McCone, Nitze, and Taylor were hawks, arguing for an air strike. Then Dillon swung to the doves. Rusk took neither one side nor the other. McNamara stayed close by Robert, who spoke with great fluency about keeping options open. Dillon, the new convert, argued that they could operate the blockade and then, afterwards, if need be send in the air strike. In other words, they could do both, but only in that order. Around ten o'clock that night the President telephoned and asked them all over to tell him what they had come up with.

More farce ensued. There were still newsmen hanging around the State Department. A motorcade of limousines would draw attention to the senior officials leaving. Nine Ex-Comm members squashed into one limousine. There was no room for the Assistant Secretary of State for Inter-American Affairs, Edwin M. Martin. He volunteered to walk the ten blocks to the White House in the crisp, clear autumn night. As the limousine drew away someone asked "What happens if we get into a collision?"

They waved at Ed Martin as they passed him on the sidewalk. Someone else said, "There's always Ed."

At the White House, the President listened to the discussion and could tell that the general view was in support of the blockade or what was also known as quarantine.

Next morning the President left Washington for Cleveland for another round of campaign appearances; business as usual. But he had been drawn aside before departure to hear out the Joint Chiefs of Staff, who were begging for an invasion or an air strike. He also heard out Acheson who, more sharply than ever, was opposing the naval blockade. Bundy now did not much like either of the choices. And Dean Rusk was still uncertain.

JFK went to Cleveland and then on to Chicago. The others once again reviewed the two options. Those in favor of the air strike received a written argument from Bundy. Bobby Kennedy and Acheson sparred with each other. RFK telephoned his brother to persuade him to come back to Washington as soon as possible. JFK agreed and thought up an excuse with O'Donnell.

O'Donnell told the baffled Press Secretary that the President might have to catch a cold in the head the next day.

Ex-Comm broke up for the night. Dean Acheson felt that he no longer had a contribution to make and left for a weekend at his farm at Sandy Spring, Maryland.

The next morning, Saturday, October 20, Salinger was summoned urgently to the President's suite in the Sheraton-Blackstone Hotel in Chicago.

Salinger recalls:

I found JFK, still unshaven and in his pajamas, with O'Donnell, Dave Powers, and Rear Admiral George G. Burkley, the White House physician. The President was playing it straight.

"I have a temperature and a cold," he told me. 'You had better go back downstairs and tell the press I'm returning to Washington on the advice of Dr. Burkley." Then, as I was halfway to the door, "Wait a minute. Let's be sure we're all saying the same thing."

He then took out a piece of Sheraton-Blackstone stationery and wrote: "99.2 degrees temperature. Upper respiratory infection. Doctor says he should return to Washington." He gave it to me. "There, tell them that."

Salinger accordingly gave the press the story at 9:35 A.M. and an hour and a half later the President was on the way back to Washington.

Salinger said:

"Mr President, you don't have that bad a cold, do you?"

"I've had worse."

"Then there's something else?"

His unprintable answer sent a chill through me.

We were back at the White House at one-thirty. As we left the helicopter, JFK took my arm.

"You'll be around?" I nodded.

The crucial meeting of Ex-Comm took place at the White House in a meeting room on the second floor.

McNamara spoke out firmly for the blockade. So too did Dean Rusk, who had made up his mind.

Kennedy listened carefully, then inquired about plans for the defense of Berlin if, as he suspected, the Soviets should also move in there too. Then he said he was for the blockade and that was what he would tell the world at 7:00 P.M. on Monday, the day after tomorrow.

Adlai Stevenson, who had flown in from New York, said he thought the U.S. ought to call an Emergency Session of the UN Security Council timed to coincide with the presidential address. Kennedy agreed. He also accepted the message to the Organization of American States that Ed Martin had prepared.

Pierre Salinger (right) makes the announcement on October 27, 1962, that the same evening President Kennedy will address the Nation on a matter of the "highest national urgency."

Stevenson still pushed for some form of diplomatic solution, a deal. Perhaps it might be suggested that if the Soviets took their missiles out of Cuba the U.S. would take theirs away from Turkey and withdraw the U.S. Navy from Guantánamo. Ex-Comm was unanimously against a deal of this sort.

A great deal had to be achieved before the President spoke on television in forty-eight hours. Congress had to be informed as well as all United States embassies around the world. The United Kingdom, France, and West Germany needed to be told and their support gained. Both *The Washington Post* and *The New York Times,* already hot on the story, had to be asked to be discreet. (JFK telephoned Reston and Friendly himself and the papers held back information.)

The preparations continued throughout Sunday. Kennedy wrote a letter to Khrushchev that would be attached to a copy of his speech. Coded messages with instructions to ambassadors and their staffs about emergency procedures were transmitted. Salinger was finally briefed by McGeorge Bundy. The President said to Salinger, "Now aren't you glad you didn't know about this?"

Dean Acheson was commissioned to go to Europe with Walter Dowling, Ambassador to West Germany, who happened to be at home in Georgia. Unfortunately, Acheson's passport was out of date. No one thought to waive it, so the United States Passport Office in Washington had to be opened up for the first time on a Sunday. Then Acheson found he had no cash and Dowling had to lend him sixty dollars.

Acheson would explain matters to the U.S. Ambassador in London, David Bruce, and then go on to see General de Gaulle. Dowling would stop off in Germany to talk in secret with Konrad Adenauer.

Evidence of the departure of Soviet armaments from Cuba. November 6, 1962.

A USAF Boeing 707 flew the two men across the Atlantic. The small party included the CIA's Sherman Kent, who had with him photographs of the missile sites, in triplicate – a set each for Bruce, de Gaulle, and Adenauer. Three experts in photographic reconnaissance were seated behind Acheson and Dowling. Behind them were three Secret Service men carrying loaded guns.

The game of cat-and-mouse with the press continued. So, for a diversion, it was arranged that Averell Harriman, Assistant Secretary of State for Eastern Affairs, would arrive at the White House in his special car, along with the German Affairs Office's Martin Hillenbrand and the Assistant Secretary of State for Near Eastern Affairs, Phillips Talbott.

Ex-Comm reviewed the drafts of Kennedy's Monday speech prepared by Theodore Sorensen. It was agreed that the purpose of the United States must be stated clearly. The missiles must be removed. There must be no more shipments.

President Kennedy informed the British Ambassador to Washington, David Ormsby-Gore, of the crisis. Kennedy asked his old friend what he would advise. Ormsby-Gore advised a blockade.

The President smiled and took the British Ambassador to lunch and coffee afterwards on the White House's Truman balcony. The plan was then approved by the National Security Council.

The secret communications to be dispatched around the world were prepared in the State Department under the supervision of Dean Rusk.

When they had been completed, Rusk said, "Gentlemen, by this time tomorrow we will be in a flaming crisis." That same evening, McNamara authorized the USAF in the United States to load up nuclear weapons. In England, at the Greenham Common airbase, near Newbury, Berkshire, a solitary figure waited for the Boeing 707 to land.

This was Ambassador Bruce. He had told been told to go there alone and armed. So he had borrowed a loaded handgun from one of the Marines at the Embassy in Grosvenor Square. He also brought a bottle of Scotch to Greenham Common as a gift for his old friend Acheson. Bruce was told to see Macmillan the first thing in the morning and show him the pictures.

The two men shook hands and Acheson got back into the 707 and ordered it on to Paris.

On Monday, October 22, the Congressional leaders, twenty of them in all, were summoned to see the President at the White House at 5:00 P.M.; they were brought to Washington in Air Force planes.

The meeting went unexpectedly badly. William Fulbright, chairman of the senate Foreign Relations Committee, chastised Kennedy for not invading. He agreed with the Democratic Senator from Georgia, Richard Russell. (Fulbright had been against the Bay of Pigs, and had described Castro's regime as a "thorn in the flesh . . . not a dagger in the heart.") Another congressman said he wanted the record to show that he had not been "consulted" – he had been "informed." Kennedy left the meeting furious.

Before 7:00 P.M. all the Western leaders had been informed. Only one, Canada's Prime Minister Diefenbaker, declared himself uneasy about the American plan. The rest gave their support. Promptly at 7:00 P.M. all the American TV networks broadcast Kennedy's speech:

Good evening, my fellow citizens. This Government, as promised, has maintained the closest surveillance of the Soviet military buildup on the island of Cuba. Within the past week, unmistakable evidence has established the fact that a series of offensive missile sites is now in preparation on that imprisoned island. The purpose of these bases can be none other than to provide a nuclear stike capability against the Western Hemisphere. . . .

This urgent transformation of Cuba into an important strategic base, by the presence of these large, long-range and clearly offensive weapons of sudden mass destruction, constitutes an explicit threat to the peace and security of all the Americas. . . .

The size of this undertaking makes clear that it has been planned for some months. Yet only last month, after I had made clear the distinction between any introduction of ground-to-ground missiles and the existence of defensive antiaircraft missiles, the Soviet Government publicly stated on September 11 that – and I quote – "The armaments and military equipment sent to Cuba are designed exclusively for defensive purposes," and – and I quote the Soviet Government – "There is no need for the Soviet Government to shift its weapons for a retaliatory blow to any other country, for instance Cuba," and that – and I quote the government – "The Soviet Union has such powerful rockets to carry these nuclear warheads that there is no need to search for sites for them beyond the boundaries of the Soviet Union." That statement was false.

Only last Tuesday, as evidence of this rapid offensive buildup was already in my hand, Soviet Foreign Minister Gromyko told me in my office that he was instructed to make it clear once again, as he said his government had already done, that Soviet assistance to Cuba – and I quote – "pursued solely the purpose of contributing to the defense capabilities of Cuba," that – and I quote him – "training by Soviet specialists of Cuban nationals in handling defensive armaments was by no means offensive," and that "if it were otherwise," Mr. Gromyko went on, "the Soviet government would never become involved in rendering such assistance." That statement also was false. . . .

But this secret, swift and extraordinary buildup of Communist missiles, in an area well known to have a special and historical relationship to the United States and the nations of the Western Hemisphere, in violation of Soviet assurances and in defiance of American and hemispheric policy – this sudden, clandestine decision to station strategic weapons for the first time outside of Soviet soil is a deliberately provocative and unjustified change in the status quo which cannot be accepted by this country, if our courage and our commitments are ever to be trusted again by either friend or foe. . . .

Acting, therefore, in the defense of our own security and of the entire Western Hemisphere, and under the authority entrusted to me by the Constitution as endorsed by the Resolution of the Congress, I have directed that the following initial steps be taken immediately:

First, to halt this offensive buildup, a strict quarantine on all offensive military equipment under shipment to Cuba is being initiated. All ships of any kind bound for Cuba from whatever nation or port will, if found to contain cargoes of offensive weapons, be turned back. This quarantine will be extended, if needed, to other types of cargo and carriers. We are not at this time, however, denying the necessities of life as the Soviets attempted to do in their Berlin blockade of 1948.

Second, I have directed the continued and increased close surveillance of Cuba and its military buildup. The Foreign Ministers of the OAS, in their communiqué of October 6, rejected secrecy on such matters in this hemisphere. Should these offensive military preparations continue, thus increasing the threat to the hemisphere, further action will be justified. I have directed the armed forces to prepare for any eventualities; and I trust that, in the interest of both the Cuban people and the Soviet technicians at the sites, the hazards to all concerned of continuing this threat will be recognized.

Third, it shall be the policy of this nation to regard any nuclear missile launched from Cuba against any nation in the Western Hemisphere as an attack by the Soviet Union on the United States, requiring a full retaliatory response upon the Soviet Union.

Fourth, as a necessary military precaution, I have reinforced our base at Guantánamo, evacuated today the dependents of our personnel there and ordered additional military units to be on a standby alert basis.

Fifth, we are calling tonight for an immediate meeting of the Organ of Consultation under the Organization of American States, to consider this threat to hemispheric security and to invoke Articles 6 and 8 of the Rio Treaty in support of all necessary action. The United Nations Charter allows for regional security arrangements, and the nations of this hemisphere decided long ago against the military presence of outside powers. Our other allies around the world have also been alerted.

Sixth, under the Charter of the United Nations, we are asking tonight that an emergency meeting of the Security Council be convoked without delay to take action against this latest Soviet threat to world peace. Our resolution will call for the prompt dismantling and withdrawal of all offensive weapons in Cuba, under the supervision of UN observers, before the quarantine can be lifted.

Seventh and finally, I call upon Chairman Khrushchev to halt and eliminate this clandestine, reckless, and provocative threat to world peace and to stable relations between our two nations. I call upon him further to abandon this course of world domination, and to join in an historic effort to end the perilous arms race and transform the history of man. He has an opportunity now to move the world back from the abyss of destruction, by returning to his government's own words that it had no need to station missiles outside its own territory and withdrawing these weapons from Cuba, by refraining from any action which will widen or deepen the present crisis, and then by participating in a search for peaceful and permanent solutions.

This nation is prepared to present its case against the Soviet threat to peace, and our own proposals for a peaceful world, at any time and in any forum. . . .

But it is difficult to settle or even discuss these problems in an atmosphere of intimidation. That is why this latest Soviet threat, or any other threat which is made either independently or in response to our actions this week, must and will be met with determination. Any hostile move anywhere in the world against the safety and freedom of peoples to whom we are committed, including in particular the brave people of West Berlin, will be met by whatever action is needed.

Finally, I want to say a few words to the captive people of Cuba, to whom this speech is being directly carried by special radio facilities. I speak to you as a friend, as one who knows your deep attachment to your fatherland, as one who shares your aspirations for liberty and justice for all. And I have watched and the American people have watched with deep sorrow how your nationalist revolution was betrayed, and how your fatherland fell under foreign domination. Now your leaders are no longer Cuban leaders inspired by Cuban ideals. They are puppets and agents of an international conspiracy which has turned Cuba against your friends and neighbors in the Americas, and turned it into the first Latin-American country to become a target for nuclear war – the first Latin-American country to have these weapons on its soil.

These new weapons are not in your interest. They contribute nothing to your peace and well-being. They can only undermine it. But this country has no wish to cause you to suffer or to impose any system upon you. We know that your lives and land are being used as pawns by those who deny you freedom. . . .

Our goal is not the victory of might, but the vindication of right; not peace at the expense of freedom, but both peace and freedom here in this hemisphere, and, we hope, around the world. God willing, that goal will be achieved.

Tuesday, October 23. It was another spectacularly golden fall day in Washington. Rusk woke up and telephoned George Ball:

"We have won a considerable victory," said Rusk.

"We have?" Ball answered, blearily from his office, where he had slept all night.

"You and I," said Rusk confidently, "are still alive."

The blockade would now go into effect in twenty-four hours.

In the Atlantic twenty-five Soviet freighters were heading for Cuba. There was a Soviet submarine force in the Caribbean. Still, the Soviet Union denied the existence of the aggressive missiles. Again, Robert Kennedy saw Ambassador Dobrynin; again, the Ambassador denied the presence of the missiles.

At 10:00 A.M. on Wednesday, October 24, the blockade went into effect. The ships of the U.S. Navy were positioned five hundred miles from the coast of Cuba, out of range of the Soviet MIG jet fighters on the Cuban mainland. The U.S. Naval force was under the command of Vice-Admiral Alfred Gustave "Corky" Ward. His wait for the Soviet freighters carrying nuclear missiles would be short. The fateful first sighting could take place within two to three hours. The Navy's carrier-based jets swept the ocean, watching and waiting.

In Moscow, an exhausted Khrushchev called upon a visiting businessman, William Knox, a friend of Dean Rusk's and now president of the Westinghouse Corporation, to convey a message home. Khrushchev admitted to Knox that the U.S.S.R. had missiles in Cuba. More were on the way. The Soviet Union would fire the missiles if it chose to. Endlessly, Khrushchev attacked Kennedy. "How can I deal with a man who is younger than my son?" Knox agreed to give the garbled message to the White House when he got to Washington next day.

But before Knox reached home, news reached the President and his advisors in the White House that a Soviet submarine had taken up a position close to two of the Soviet freighters, *Gagarin* and *Komiles*. It was decided that the aircraft carrier *Essex* should dispatch helicopters with anti-submarine weapons. *The Essex* would then send a sonar signal to the Soviet submarine, telling it to surface and reveal its identity. If it refused, depth charges would

During the Cuban missile crisis, the U.S.S. *Barry (foreground)* draws alongside the Soviet freighter *Anosov*.

be dropped into the sea around the submarine and it would be forced to come up.

"I think," said Robert Kennedy, in *Thirteen Days*, that "these few minutes were the time of gravest concern for the President . . ."

Was the world on the brink of a holocaust? Was it our error? A mistake? Was there something further that should have been done? Or not done? His hand went up to his face and covered his mouth. He opened and closed his fist. His face seemed drawn, his eyes pained, almost gray. We stared at each other across the table. For a few fleeting seconds, it was almost as though no one else was there and he was no longer the President.

Inexplicably, I thought of when he was ill and almost died; when he lost his child; when he learned that our oldest brother had been killed; of personal times of strain and hurt. The voices droned on, but I didn't seem to hear anything until I heard the President say: "Isn't there some way we can avoid having our first exchange with a Russian submarine – almost anything but that?"

"No, there's too much danger to our ships. There is no alternative," said McNamara. "Our commanders have been instructed to avoid hostilities if at all possible, but this is what we must be prepared for, and this is what we must expect."

We had come to the time of final decision.

At 10:25 A.M. a messenger brought the news to McCone that it seemed some of the Soviet ships had "stopped dead in the water."

Rusk turned to Bundy and said, "We're eyeball to eyeball and I think the other fellow just blinked."

McNamara went with Roswell Gilpatric to visit the Navy's control center in the Pentagon. There was an acid confrontation with Admiral George W. Anderson, who was in charge. McNamara asked the admiral questions, and the admiral did not want the rest of his staff to hear all the answers. He drew McNamara off to one side and McNamara at once asked if every U.S. destroyer had someone on board who spoke Russian. Anderson said he was not sure. McNamara told the admiral to find out. One authority has it that McNamara then asked the admiral what would happen if a Soviet captain refused to tell an American boarding party what his ship was carrying. Apparently, at this point, the admiral waved a copy of the U.S. Manual of Naval Regulations at McNamara and said: "It's all in there."

McNamara exploded: "I don't give a damn what John Paul Jones would have done. I want to know what you are going to do. Now."

"Now, Mr. Secretary," countered the Admiral, "if you and your deputy will go back to your offices, the Navy will run the blockade."

McNamara turned on his heel and left.

In Cuba, the pace of work on the missile sites speeded up, and bombers were made ready on the Cuban airfields.

Thursday, October 25, and no break in the tension, other than the remarkable televised performance of Adlai Stevenson at the

United Nations. The Soviet Ambassador to the UN, Valerian Zorin, challenged Stevenson to come up with evidence that the Soviet Union had prepared missiles in Cuba. Stevenson called for the right to reply and got it. The confrontation was one of Stevenson's greatest moments.

STEVENSON: Well, let me say something to you, Mr. Ambassador, we do have the evidence. We have it, and it is clear and incontrovertible. And let me say something else. Those weapons must be taken out of Cuba. . . . You, the Soviet Union, have created this new danger – not the United States. . . . Finally, Mr. Zorin, I remind you that the other day you did not deny the existence of these weapons. But today, again if I heard you correctly, you now say that they do not exist, or that we haven't proved they exist. All right, sir, let me ask you one simple question. Do you, Ambassador Zorin, deny that the U.S.S.R. has placed and is placing medium and intermediate-range missiles and sites in Cuba? Yes or no? Don't wait for the translation – yes or no?

ZORIN: I am not in an American courtroom, sir, and therefore I do not wish to answer a question that is put to me in the fashion in which a prosecutor puts his questions. In due course, sir, you will have your answer.

STEVENSON: You are in the courtroom of world opinion right now, and you can answer yes or no. You have denied that they exist, and I want to know whether I have understood you correctly.

ZORIN: Continue with your statement. You will have your answer in due course.

STEVENSON: I am prepared to wait for your answer until hell freezes over, if that's your decision. And I am also prepared to present the evidence in this room.

Then Stevenson had the photographs on the easels behind him uncovered. Huge blowups of the sites. Zorin said the photographs were ridiculous.

STEVENSON: We know the facts, and so do you, sir, and we are ready to talk about them. Our job here is not to score debating points. Our job, Mr. Zorin, is to save the peace. And if you are ready to try, we are.

The United States released fifty thousand copies of the photographs worldwide while this confrontation was taking place.

The next morning, the American destroyer that bore the name of the President's older brother who had died in the war, *Joseph P. Kenndy, Jr.*, stopped the Lebanese-registered and Panamanian-owned freighter *Marucla*. The *Marucla*'s captain responded to the "Oscar November" flag ordering the ship to heave-to and stop. The American boarding party inspected the *Marucla*'s cargo and found nothing untoward. The ship was allowed to go on to Cuba.

In Washington, Robert Kennedy again confronted Ambassador Dobrynin. He told Dobrynin that the United States would wait no longer than Sunday morning – forty-eight hours.

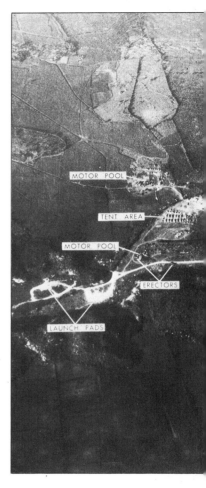

At the time of this photograph, October 17, 1962, the construction of this missile site at Sagua la Grande, Cuba, was essentially complete.

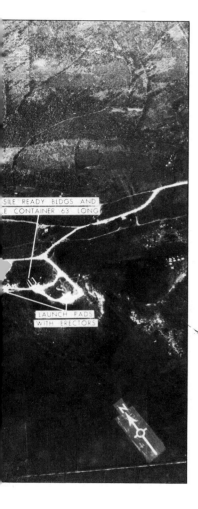

SILE READY BLDGS AND
E CONTAINER 63 LONG

LAUNCH PADS
WITH ERECTORS

N

Also in Washington, ABC-TV's John Scali received a telephone call.

Scali's caller was Alexander Fomin, ostensibly a Soviet Embassy counselor. Scali was eating a bologna sandwich. Fomin asked Scali to have lunch with him instead. It was urgent. The Russian was insistent.

Scali went to the Occidental restaurant and found Fomin waiting there. Fomin, who Scali knew was a KGB colonel, was in an uncharacteristic state of nerves. He had a message for Scali; or rather, he wanted Scali's views. Would the State Department agree to the missile sites being dismantled and shipped out of Cuba under the supervision of the United Nations? Would the State Department be pleased to learn that Fidel Castro would offer a promise never to accept offensive weapons again? Would the United States, in return promise not to launch an invasion against Cuba?

Scali said he really could not be sure.

Fomin said that if Stevenson were to negotiate at the UN on these terms, he would find Ambassador Zorin amenable. Astonished, Scali listened to Fomin begging him to communicate this offer to the State Department. He told Roger Hilsman, head of intelligence at the State Department, about Fomin's approach. Hilsman was understandably skeptical. So they both went to see Dean Rusk.

Rusk told Scali to go back and see Fomin again and to take the following message:

I have reason to believe that the United States Government sees real possibilities in this and supposes that representatives of the two governments could work this matter out with U Thant and with each other. My impression is, however, that time is very urgent.

Scali told Fomin to meet him shortly after 7:30 P.M. at the Statler Hilton Hotel's coffee shop. This was near the Soviet Embassy. Fomin asked where the reply had come from. Scali told him it had come from "the highest sources." The Soviet KGB colonel left the coffee shop and walked back to the Soviet Embassy.

Even before the second Scali-Fomin meeting, a verbose and emotional letter was being received over the State Department's teletype link to the U.S. embassy in Moscow. It reflected all the terms that Alexander Fomin had given to Scali over their lunch at the Occidental a few hours before. Khrushchev said:

If you have not lost your self-control, and sensibly conceive what this might lead to, then, Mr. President, we and you ought not now to pull on the ends of the rope in which you have tied the knot of war, because the more we pull, the tighter the knot will be tied. And a moment may come when the knot will be tied so tight that even he who tied it will not have the strength to untie it, and then it will be necessary to cut that knot; and what that would mean is not for me to explain to you, because you yourself understand perfectly of what terrible forces our countries dispose.

Consequently, if there is no intention to tighten that knot and thereby doom the world to the catastrophe of thermonuclear war, then let us not only relax the forces pulling on the ends of the rope, let us take measures to untie that knot. We are ready for this.

The next morning, Saturday, October 27, Kennedy met with Ex-Comm. He was pleased that Khrushchev did not insist upon the Americans withdrawing their Jupiter missiles from Turkey.

And yet McCone, giving his usual account of the latest secret intelligence, said that there was no letup in the preparation of the missile sites. Worse followed.

Radio Moscow now broadcast a second letter from Chairman Khrushchev. He was now insisting on the U.S. missiles being taken out of Turkey. At the same time as this new message was coming through, J. Edgar Hoover telephoned Robert Kennedy to say that Soviet diplomats in New York were clearing their offices and disposing of secret documents. Then news reached the White House that a U-2 had been shot down over Cuba by a Soviet missile. The sites were now working and ready.

Which letter should the President answer now?

It was Robert Kennedy who proposed calmly that the President answer the first and ignore the second. Ex-Comm then broke up into groups and replies were drafted by Ball, Bundy, Thompson, and Rusk. Robert Kennedy did not approve of any of them. "If you can do better, then you do it," JFK told his brother.

The letter was drafted with the help of Sorensen and dispatched just after 8:00 P.M. to Khrushchev. Pierre Salinger simultaneously handed out to the press copies of the letter accepting the Soviet proposals.

That night, as Ex-Comm once more adjourned, the President was heard to say, "Now it can go either way."

The next day, Sunday, October 28, George Ball and Robert McNamara hurried into the White House. It was a spectacularly beautiful autumn morning. McNamara turned to Ball and said the October sun reminded him of the painting by Georgia O'Keeffe "that has a rose growing out of an ox skull."

Almost at the same time that Ex-Comm assembled, Radio Moscow began to broadcast Khrushchev's answer to Kennedy's letter:

In order to eliminate as rapidly as possible the conflict which endangers the cause of peace, to give an assurance to all people who crave peace, and to reassure the American people who, I am certain, also want peace, as do the people of the Soviet Union, the Soviet Government, in addition to earlier instructions on the discontinuation of further work on weapons construction sites, has given a new order to dismantle the arms which you have described as offensive, and to crate and return them to the Soviet Union.

Kennedy accepted and commented upon Khrushchev's comments about nuclear disarmament. He wrote to Moscow:

I agree with you that we must devote urgent attention to the problem of disarmament, as it relates to the whole world and also to critical areas.

Perhaps now, as we step back from danger, we can together make real progress in this vital field. I think we should give priority to questions relating to the proliferation of nuclear weapons, on earth and in outer space, and to the great effort for a nuclear test ban.

That night, RFK went to the White House and talked alone with his brother in the Oval Office. He recalled:

While I was there, he placed telephone calls to former Presidents Truman and Eisenhower. As I was leaving, he said, making reference to Abraham Lincoln, "This is the night I should go to the theater."
I said, "If you go, I want to go with you."

He left his brother alone, seated at his desk, writing a letter.

The letter was to the widow of Major Rudolph Anderson Jr., the widow of the U-2 pilot who had been shot down over Cuba the day before.

The treaty that banned nuclear testing in the atmosphere was signed in Moscow on August 5, 1963. The signatories were Andrei Gromyko, Lord Home, and Dean Rusk. The path to the agreement had been tortuous.

President Kennedy signs the instruments of ratification for the Nuclear Test Ban Treaty, July 10, 1963. Shortly after this photograph was taken, JFK told his friend Dave Powers that this was the happiest day of his life.

Chapter 10

Visions of Peace and Violence

I am happy to join with you today in what will go down in history as the greatest demonstration for freedom in the history of our nation.

Five score years ago, a great American, in whose symbolic shadow we stand today, signed the Emancipation Proclamation. This momentous decree came as a great beacon light of hope to millions of Negro slaves who had been seared in the flames of withering injustice. It came as a joyous daybreak to end the long night of their captivity.

But one hundred years later, the Negro still is not free. One hundred years later, the life of the Negro is still sadly crippled by the manacles of segregation and the chains of discrimination. One hundred years later the Negro lives on a lonely island of poverty in the midst of a vast ocean of material prosperity. One hundred years later the Negro is still languishing in the corners of American society and finds himself in exile in his own land.

So we've come here today to dramatize a shameful condition. In a sense, we've come to our nation's capital to cash a check. When the architects of our republic wrote the magnificent words of the Constitution and the Declaration of Independence, they were signing a promissory note to which every American was to fall heir. This note was a promise that all men – yes, black men as well as white men – would be guaranteed the unalienable rights of life, liberty, and the pursuit of happiness.

It is obvious today that America has defaulted on this promissory note insofar as her citizens of color are concerned. Instead of honoring this sacred obligation, America has given the Negro people a bad check. A check which has come back marked "insufficient funds."

But we refuse to believe that the bank of justice is bankrupt. . . .

There will be neither rest nor tranquility in America until the Negro is granted his citizenship rights. The whirlwind of revolt will continue to shake the foundations of our nation until the bright day of justice emerges. But there is something that I must say to my people who stand on the warm threshold which leads into the palace of justice. In the process of gaining our rightful place, we must not be guilty of wrongful deeds. Let us not seek to satisfy our thirst for freedom by drinking from the cup of bitterness and hatred.

We must forever conduct our struggle on the high plane of dignity and discipline. We must not allow our creative protest to degenerate into physical violence. Again and again we must rise to the majestic heights of meeting physical force with soul force. The marvelous new militancy, which has engulfed the Negro community, must not lead us to a distrust of all white people, for many of our white brothers, as evidenced by their presence here today, have come to realize that their destiny is tied up with our destiny. . . .

So even though we face the difficulties of today and tomorrow, I still have a dream. It is a dream deeply rooted in the American dream. I have a

Dr. Martin Luther King, Jr., acknowledges the crowds at the Lincoln Memorial on the day of the great march on Washington, August 28, 1963.

dream that one day this nation will rise up and live out the true meaning of its creed. We hold these truths to be self-evident that all men are created equal.

I have a dream that one day on the red hills of Georgia, sons of former slaves and sons of former slave owners will be able to sit down together at the table of brotherhood. I have a dream. That one day – even the state of Mississippi, a state sweltering with the heat of injustice; sweltering with the heat of oppression – will be transformed into an oasis of freedom and justice. I have a dream. That my four little children will one day live in a nation where they will not be judged by the color of their skin but by the content of their character. I have a dream today.

I have a dream that one day down in Alabama, with its vicious racists, with its Governor having his lips dripping with the words of interposition and nullification, one day right there in Alabama, little black boys and black girls will be able to join hands with little white boys and white girls as sisters and brothers. I have a dream today. . . .

Let freedom ring, and when this happens – when we allow freedom to ring, when we let it ring from every village and every hamlet, from every state and every city, we will be able to speed up that day when all of God's children – black men and white men, Jews and Gentiles, Protestants and Catholics – will be able to join hands and sing in the words of the old Negro spiritual: Free at last. Free at last. Thank God A'mighty, we are free at last!

(Dr. Martin Luther King, Jr., Washington, D.C., August 28, 1963)

Two thousand years ago the proudest boast was "Civitas Romanus sum." Today, in the world of freedom, the proudest boast is "Ich bin ein Berliner."

There are many people in the world who really don't understand, or say they don't, what is the great issue between the free world and the Communist world. Let them come to Berlin. There are some who say that Communism is the wave of the future. Let them come to Berlin. And there are some who say in Europe and elswhere we can work with the Communists. Let them come to Berlin. And there are even a few who say that it is true that Communism is an evil system, but it permits us to make economic progress. "Lasst sie nach Berlin kommen."

Freedom has many difficulties and democracy is not perfect, but we have never had to put a wall up to keep our people in, to prevent them from leaving us. I want to say, on behalf of my countrymen who live many miles away on the other side of the Atlantic, who are far distant from you, that they take the greatest pride that they have been able to share with you, even from a distance, the story of the last eighteen years. I know of no town, no city, that has been besieged for eighteen years that still lives with the vitality and the force, and the hope and the determination of the city of West Berlin. While the wall is the most obvious and vivid demonstration of the failures of the Communist system, for all the world to see, we take no satisfaction in it, for it is an offense not only against history but an offense against humanity, separating families, dividing husbands and

Above JFK with Willy Brandt, Mayor of West Berlin, at the Brandenburg Gate in Berlin in June 1963. The East Berlin authorities covered the arches with red cloth to prevent the President from seeing into East Berlin.

Below left JFK, Willy Brandt, and Konrad Adenauer, the West German Chancellor in Berlin, June 26, 1963.
Below and **right** "Ich bin ein Berliner."

wives and brothers and sisters, and dividing a people who wish to be joined together.

What is true of this city is true of Germany – real, lasting peace in Europe can never be assured as long as one German out of four is denied the elementary right of free men, and that is to make a free choice. In eighteen years of peace and good faith, this generation of Germans has earned the right to be free, including the right to unite their families and their nation in lasting peace with good will to all people. You live in a defended island of freedom, but your life is part of the main. So let me ask you, as I close, to lift your eyes beyond the dangers of today to the hopes of tomorrow, beyond the freedom merely of this city of Berlin, or your country of Germany, to the advance of freedom everywhere, beyond the wall to the day of peace with justice, beyond yourselves and ourselves to all mankind. Freedom is indivisible, and when one man is enslaved, all are not free. When all are free, then we can look forward to that day when this city will be joined as one – and this country, and this great continent of Europe – in a peaceful and hopeful glow. When that day finally comes, as it will, the people of West Berlin can take sober satisfaction in the fact that they were in the front lines for almost two decades.

All free men, wherever they may live, are citizens of Berlin, and, therefore, as a free man, I take pride in the words "Ich bin ein Berliner."
(John F. Kennedy's speech in Rudolf Wilde Platz, Berlin, Germany, June 26, 1963)

A police riot tank stands by as a black housing project is destroyed by fire after a night of rioting, looting, and arson. Birmingham, Alabama, May 11, 1963.

The temperature of violence in the United States rose continuously throughout 1963. "I can well understand," said President Kennedy, "why the Negroes of Birmingham are tired of being asked to be patient." So could the rest of the world when they saw newspaper photographs of Bull Connor's police dogs ripping the legs of black women and dispersing black demonstrators with fire fighters' hoses. Many whites in the south focused their burning resentment upon the Attorney General.

The mayor of Birmingham said, "I hope that every drop of blood that's spilled he tastes in his throat, and I hope he chokes on it." Black homes were firebombed. The riots continued. President Kennedy ordered military reinforcements to Birmingham. Governor Wallace spoke of a "military dictatorship." The blacks marched in Alabama, Georgia, North and South Carolina, Tennessee, Louisiana, Mississippi, and Illinois. Throughout the summer, between thirteen and fifteen thousand blacks were sent to prison in the Southern states. Robert Kennedy sought to reason with George Wallace, to no avail at all, and he sent his assistants South to aid the peaceful entry of blacks onto campuses. Then Medgar Evers was murdered in Jackson, Mississippi. King spoke in Washington to an audience of almost a quarter of a million. But his peaceful vision of integration was not enough. Though he might gain his dream by peaceful means, others thought the only way to wake up out of the nightmare of inequality, poverty, and injustice was violence. The same mayor of Birmingham who wished that Robert Kennedy might choke on blood said:

Martin Luther King is a revolutionary. The Nigger King ought to be investigated by the Attorney General. This nigger has got the blessing of the Attorney General and the White House.

Right Dr. Martin Luther King in Birmingham, Alabama, May 9, 1963.
Below JFK arrives at Otis Air Force Base Hospital to visit his wife. August 13, 1963. Their son Patrick had died two days after his birth on August 9.

King was indeed investigated – by J. Edgar Hoover's FBI, which seemed to assume King was a Communist. And the investigation was not prevented by Robert Kennedy. Perhaps the Attorney General thought that if Hoover investigated King, the black leader would, through innocence of whatever charges Hoover was trying to make, be confirmed in an even stronger position as a spokesman of nonviolence and decency. But it was a misjudged authorization.

King had detractors among blacks as well. Malcolm X said in Washington, "You need somebody who is going to fight. You don't need any kneeling in or crawling in."

It was a hot and violent summer – the summer of 1963.

Kennedy visited Europe and spoke at the Berlin Wall in June to a vast crowd of admiring and tearful Germans: "Ich bin ein Berliner."

In August, Jacqueline Kennedy gave birth to her third child and second son. His name was Patrick Bouvier Kennedy. He weighed four pounds and ten ounces at birth and was five and a half weeks premature. During the afternoon of August 9, the child died.

Profoundly affected by this tragedy, the President and his wife returned to Washington.

JFK receives the leaders of the march on Washington, August 28, 1963.

Two weeks later he watched the great march on Washington and listened to Dr. King's speech. Afterwards, he met Dr. King and his associates at the White House telling them that he also had a dream. But that day belonged to Dr. King. He had been introduced as a "philosopher of a nonviolent system of behavior . . . seeking to bring about social change for the advancement of justice and freedom and human dignity . . . the moral leader of our nation." The President watched the events on television.

In October, Jacqueline accepted an invitation from Aristotle Onassis to cruise in the Aegean. She went with her sister, Lee Radziwill, and came home, loaded with gifts, on October 17.

The President asked her if she would accompany him on a trip to Texas the next month. He was going to Texas to campaign and to settle a squabble between two of the state's leading Democrats, conservative Governor John Connally and the more liberal Senator Ralph Yarborough. It was important to secure a united Democratic Party in Texas before the campaign got underway in earnest the following year.

The President woke in suite 850 of the Hotel Texas in Fort Worth on Friday, November 22, to look out at a rainy day. Over breakfast he discussed the Yarborough – Connally squabble with Kenneth O'Donnell. Yarborough was even refusing to ride in the same car as Lyndon Johnson. The President said it was ridiculous. Yarborough would, he told O'Donnell, either ride with Johnson or he would walk. Then JFK went to his wife's room, looked out the windows and saw more than two thousand people in the parking lot where he was soon due to speak briefly. He left his wife alone to breakfast and to dress in a suit of raspberry pink with a dark purple collar and a small pillbox hat.

JFK and Jacqueline arrive in Dallas, November 22, 1963.

Top, left to right JFK prior to appearing before the press and television cameras; LBJ and JFK across the table; RFK and JFK in the Oval Office.
Below far left JFK with Walter Rostow, Assistant Secretary of State.
Below left JFK used the telephone more than any president of modern times.
Right JFK facing the press, February 21, 1963. Pierre Salinger is on his left.

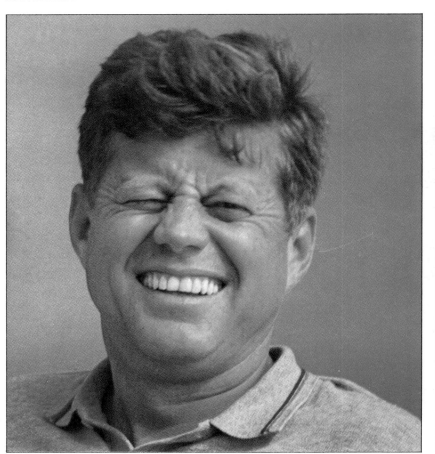

A relaxed JFK at Cape Cod in the summer of 1963.

The President, surrounded by Secret Service men and police, and accompanied by LBJ and Lady Bird, left the hotel and crossed through the cheering crowd to the parking lot. He climbed up onto the truck and moved toward the microphones, where he said:

Mr. Vice-President, Jim Wright, Governor, Senator Yarborough, Mr. Buck, ladies and gentlemen. There are no faint hearts in Fort Worth, and I appreciate you being here this morning. . . .

Someone called out: "Where's Jackie?"

Mrs. Kennedy is organizing herself. It takes longer. But, of course, she looks better than we do when she does it.

The crowd laughed and clapped.

But we appreciate your welcome. . . .

He spoke of Fort Worth as "a great Western city, the defense of the West, cattle, oil, and all the rest." He was rambling. He tried to save the speech with the Kennedy rhythm. "It has believed in strength in this city, and strength in this state, and strength in this country. . . ."
He spoke of the thriving economy, of space, of the vital interests of the United States. He gained his applause.

And in the final analysis, the strength depends upon the willingness of the citizens of the United States to assume the burdens of leadership.

The crowd had heard it all before, but it was different to hear and see it so close.

I know one place where they are, here in this rain, in Fort Worth, in Texas, in the United States. We are going forward. Thank you.

The shouts were deafening. Rebel yells. Screams. Whistles.
Back in the hotel he and Jacqueline attended a breakfast for the local dignitaries of the Democratic Party. When his turn came to speak, JFK moved to the lectern, smiled, and began:

Two years ago I introduced myself in Paris by saying that I was the man who had accompanied Mrs. Kennedy to Paris. I am getting somewhat that same sensation as I travel around Texas.

Jacqueline restrained a laugh with her white-gloved hand.

Nobody wonders what Lyndon and I wear. . . .

He spoke generally about the defense budget, about the confrontation in Cuba, about Vietnam.

I am confident, as I look at the future, that our chances for security, our

chances for peace, are better than they have been in the past. And the reason is because we are stronger. And with that strength is a determination to not only maintain the peace, but also the vital interests of the United States. To that cause Texas and the United States are committed.

Above The presidential limousine in Dallas, November 22, 1963.
Right One minute before the assassination of President Kennedy.

The presidential luggage was carted out of the hotel, and as the motorcade was assembled, Senator Yarborough climbed into Lyndon Johnson's car as he had been told.

At Carswell Air Force Base, the President smiled and waved to well-wishers before boarding Air Force One. Among the passengers were the faithfuls: O'Donnell and O'Brien; Dave Powers; Mary Gallagher, the First Lady's personal secretary; Mrs. Lincoln; Malcolm Kilduff; Dr. Burkley, the President's doctor. Senator Yarborough and Governor Connally were there with Mrs. Connally.

Lyndon and Lady Bird Johnson were in the vice-presidential Boeing 707, Air Force Two.

Air Force One was in crisp condition. It had been recently redesigned by the designer of the Coca-Cola bottle, Raymond Loewy. The jet swept down the runway and into the sky, bound for Dallas. The temperature there was 76 degrees. The day was fine and clear. There would be no need to fix the bullet-proof glass-bubble top to the presidential limousine.

Air Force One landed at Love Field at 11:39 A.M. local time.

Again there were crowds waiting. Cheering. Smiling. Waving. And the cries of "*Jacke-ee, Jacke-ee, Jacke-ee!*"

Everyone wanted to be in the presidential motorcade. There were twenty-four cars lined up. The President and Mrs. Kennedy climbed into the Lincoln with Governor and Mrs. Connally. The police motorcycle outriders started their engines.

At 11:55 A.M. the motorcade swept away from Love Field bound for Dallas.

Following the Kennedys' car were four police motorcycles. After them came the limousine packed with Secret Service men. Kinney was driving. Roberts was in charge of the radio. Ready was on the running board at one side, and Hill, whose task was the protection of Mrs. Kennedy, was on the other. The rest included agents McIntyre, Landis, Bennett, and Hickey. An automatic rifle was discreetly hidden. After the Secret Service came the Johnsons in another open Lincoln. And so on down the line: Lincolns, Chevrolets, a Mercury station wagon. The whole procession stretched away behind the presidential Lincoln for more than half a mile. Dr. Burkley was fifteen cars away from the President.

The estimate was that some 250,000 people had come out to have a look at the Kennedys in Dallas.

MR. PRESIDENT PLEASE STOP AND SHAKE OUR HANDS, JFK read on a banner as the Lincoln passed Craddock Park.

"Stop here," he told his driver, Bill Greer.

The President leaned out and shook the hands of some children. It was now past noon and the air was cooler.

"Thank you. Thank you, Thank you," the President said, smiling at the crowds.

Into North Dallas, the greener area, where there were fewer crowds. Jacqueline started to put on her sunglasses. The President asked her not to. He turned to wave at a group of nuns. Then he turned to John Connally. "How do things look in Texas?"

Connally told him that the *Houston Chronicle* was publishing a new poll the next day."

"What will it show?"

"You're carrying the state. It'll be a close election."

Across Harwood. Toward Main. At the top of Main Street. Police Headquarters. Field Street. The cheers were enormous. The outriders fell back into position. On to Dealey Plaza.

Five more minutes, and it would be time for lunch.

A schoolboy waved. President Kennedy raised his hand as though to catch a shattering, harsh, fractured noise.

He was trying to lift his hands to his face. . . .

"Hit." "Get down." A siren rose and drowned out the shouts. Two lumps from the President's head split away. One turned into blood and splashed an outrider. Blood spray filled the rear of the car.

"*Parkland . . . ten four. Stand by. The President has been hit.*" The radio instructions were barked out.

Clinton Hill, Secret Service agent, hurled himself onto the back of the presidential Lincoln. Jacqueline had turned, her face contorted. Half standing-up she reached out and held Clint Hill's wrist. The Lincoln accelerated, seeming to rise up as it surged forward.

Hill looked down into the rear of the car. Much of the President's head was missing. His blood streamed across seats, clothes, hands. Governor Connally was unconscious. He too had been hit.

In just under six minutes, they reached the hospital.

Dallas, November 22, 1963. The presidential motorcade turned left at the corner of Elm and Houston streets. Thereafter the route would lead down to an underpass. At the head of the motorcade were the police motorcycles and then, in a black Lincoln, President and Mrs. Kennedy with John Connally, Governor of Texas, and his wife.

Passing the Texas School Book Depository, the President turned right to wave to someone as a bullet struck him in the neck. The President slumped forward beside his wife. A second shot struck Governor Connally. Mrs. Kennedy reached out to help her husband when a third shot fired at a range of 250 feet hit the President in the rear part of his head. Mrs. Kennedy shouted "Oh, no! Oh, no!" and climbed toward the rear of the Lincoln.

Jacqueline held her husband in her arms. As the other cars from the chaotic motorcade drew up, the passengers got out and rushed toward the Lincoln.

The remains of the President's head lay in Jacqueline Kennedy's lap. Clint Hill asked her to let him help her.

She shook her head.

The stretchers came, and Governor Connally was laid on the first.

But still Mrs. Kennedy held her husband. Clint Hill took off his jacket, and Mrs. Kennedy wrapped it gently around her husband's head. The President was lifted out onto a stretcher and wheeled into the hospital.

He was taken to Trauma Room 1 and surrounded by doctors.

It was 12:55 P.M. The electrocardiograph stopped.

Jacqueline Kennedy stood at one side of the tiny room. She reached forward and touched her husband.

Dr. Burkley held the President's wrist and felt the pulse.

He turned to Mrs. Kennedy, his face wet with tears.

"The President is dead."

At 1:00 Dr. Kemp Clark, Parklands Chief neurosurgeon, pronounced the President's death to his associate, Dr. Mac Perry.

Elsewhere the Secret Service surrounded President Johnson. J. Edgar Hoover telephoned Robert Kennedy. The teletypes of United Press International and Associated Press clattered.

Now, twenty years later, few people who heard the news that Friday afternoon have forgotten precisely where they were, what they were doing, and how they learned that John Fitzgerald Kennedy was dead. It was hard to believe it.

Secret Service Agent Clinton Hill jumped from the following car and rushed to catch the presidential car. He grabbed a handle and got one foot on the bumper. Mrs. Kennedy reached toward him as he climbed aboard. The car then picked up speed and raced to Parkland Hospital.

Jacqueline Kennedy holds the flag that draped the coffin of her late husband. On the right is Robert Kennedy. President Kennedy was buried in Arlington National Cemetery. November 25, 1963.

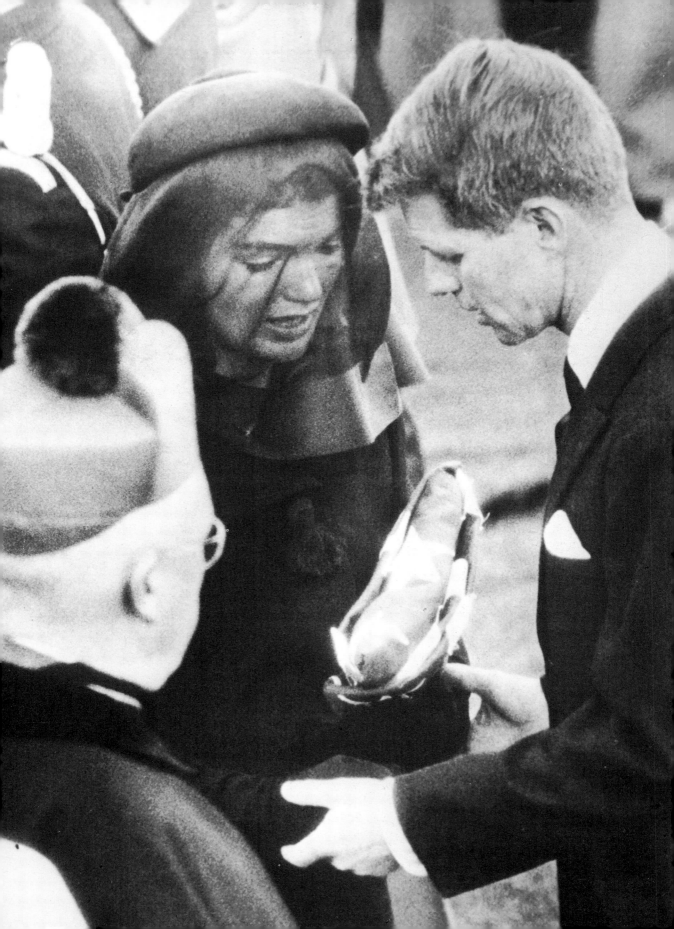